The Fourfold Path to Wholeness

Books by John G. Sullivan

The Spiral of the Seasons:
Welcoming the Gifts of Later Life
(2009)

Living Large:
Transformative Work at the Intersection
of Ethics and Spirituality
(2004)

To Come to Life More Fully:
An East West Journey
(1990)

The Fourfold Path to Wholeness

A Compass for the Heart

by John G. Sullivan, PhD

Manufactured in the United States of America.
Second Journey Publications
4 Wellesley Place
Chapel Hill, NC 27517
(919) 403-0432
www.SecondJourney.org
ISBN 978-1456449865

Design by Michael Brady Design

Photo credits: vi, Timo Laaksonen; ix–x, Stephanie Berghaeuser; pp. 15–16, Marco Ceschi; p. 32, Semantica; p. 47–48, B. Cleary; p. 64, Michael Micheletti; pp. 81–82, Janus Gawon; p. 100, Craig Goodwin.

Acknowledgments

I thank my wife, Gregg, whose presence enriches my work and my life. She is my love.

I thank my family over generations: grandparents, parents, children, grandchildren. This year, I am especially grateful for my newest grandchild, Simone Aletheia Winkelman, born July 21, 2010. I realize each day that we do indeed stand in the midst of seven generations. In all we do, may we honor the ancestors, companion our contemporaries, and serve the children.

I thank my colleagues at Second Journey, especially Bolton and Lisa Anthony who, together with graphic designer Michael Brady, saw this work into form. The book is better because of their loving care.

I thank my teaching colleagues at Tai Sophia Institute in Laurel, Maryland, especially Robert Duggan, Dianne Connelly, Anne Baker, and Helen Mitchell. They continue to shape my thinking and teaching.

I thank my colleagues at Elon University who, over decades, have supported and enhanced my work, especially the members of the Elon Philosophy Department.

I thank those who have been teachers and elders to me, especially Frederick and Claske Franck, Maynard Adams, Thomas Berry and, in the spirit, Thich Nhat Hanh and Archbishop Desmond Tutu.

I come with deep respect to the wider natural world, the Great Family of all creatures, and the Great Mystery that surrounds us. In and towards this communion, I experience gratefulness and great fullness.

I thank all those — known and unknown, named and unnamed — whose loving kindness, compassion, joy, and peace have touched me deeply.

As W. B. Yeats says in his poem "Gratitude to the Unknown Instructors":

> What they undertook to do
> they brought to pass;
> All things hung like a drop of dew
> upon a blade of grass.

— *John G. Sullivan*

Opening Words

You are a ruby embedded in granite.
How long will you pretend it isn't true?
We can see it in your eyes.
Come, return to the root of the root of your Self.[1]

— Rumi

There is a teaching — very ancient and ever new: If you would dwell more fully in the present moment, cultivate four powers: *love, compassion, joy, and peace.* Doing so will lead to a surprising recognition: They are intertwined in such a way that all four arise together. Practicing any one with open heart and mind leads to practicing the others. Each enhances each. Each balances and corrects the others, bringing the quartet back into harmony when disharmony threatens. Together, these powers constitute a Fourfold Path to health, wholeness, and holiness.

What Can We Say About This Path, This Journey?

First, *its goal is fourfold.* And that multiplicity makes it *communal.* Of old, we might have imagined a city on a mountain with four walls and four gates. The goal is partly known and partly not known. We do not have a complete blueprint for the community we seek, but we do know four of its key characteristics. We know that, at our best, we are seeking: (1) an environment that is loving and fosters love, (2) a community that is sensitive to the fragility of life and takes compassionate steps to reduce suffering, (3) a way of dwelling that is grateful for life and responds in joy, and (4) a mode of shared living that prizes inner peace and seeks harmony and reconciliation in outward affairs. This is the ancient and ever-present human dream: a loving community, a compassionate circle of care, a joyful belonging, a peaceable kingdom or commonwealth.

Second, *the path to the goal is also fourfold*. Process and goal are organically linked. Good seeds become healthy roots. Healthy roots, well tended, produce good fruits. By their fruits you shall know them; and the fruits are love, compassion, joy, and peace. Children play a game where one child thinks of something in the room. Another child tries to find it. "Hotter, hotter, hotter," say the children as their playmate comes closer. "Colder, colder, colder," say the children as their playmate moves away from the goal. So the four powers provide not only a glimpse of the goal but also a kind of compass to keep us on track. When we are acting more lovingly and compassionately, more joyfully and more peacefully, surely we are getting closer.

Third, *consider again the communal nature of the goal*. Call it the kingdom, commonwealth, or "kin-dom" (community of all our kin — humans, other animals, plants, and minerals).[2] Like Avalon, the legendary island of Arthurian lore, this communal reality is always present though hidden. The kingdom or commonwealth of all our kin is within us and also round about us. As the great sages teach, it is both *"already present in seed"* and *"not yet fully realized."*[3] In this paradox there is hope in troubled times: Because the communal life we seek is already present in seed, we can water the good seeds. We can amplify what is already in positive movement. Because the communal life we seek is already present, we need not take on the burden of "making" it appear. At times, we need only let go of our old stories and cultural certainties and see them as the illusions they are. Then the communion of all beings within us and around us will manifest to our wisdom eye. Because the manifestation of the four powers is always in process, what we do and what we release matters.

In dark and difficult times, we are called to go deeper, into the rich soil of the earth. Called to return to the root of the root of ourselves. And, if we see deeply, this includes Self, all our kin in the Circle of Life, and our Mysterious Source.

The Fourfold Path

Among our earliest ancestors, the number four pointed to wholeness. A community safe within four walls, open through four gates. Four directions in space. Four seasons in time. Four primal elements: the fire, the water, the air, and the earth.[4] To speak of "the Fourfold" is to underline this aspect, that the four are not separate but profoundly interconnected. When we practice any one of the four mindfully and insightfully, then we soon see all the others arise as well. This intertwined aspect resonated through the thinking of our early ancestors.

There are also striking modern counterparts; I offer two examples.

In the eighteenth century, William Blake writes:

> *Now I a fourfold vision see,*
> *And a fourfold vision is given to me.*

He is writing about levels of consciousness which increase from single vision (a literal way of seeing)[5] to double vision, which sees symbolically as well as literally. Next, he moves to threefold vision (the province of love, dream, imagination) and eventually to fourfold vision (where the dreamtime opens to a fuller reality than hitherto imagined, a waking dream far more real than the collective illusions of conventional life). We might say that, here, the kingdom or kin-dom is vividly before us. Furthermore, each simpler vision is taken up and resituated in fuller ways of seeing and being. The ways of seeing are intertwined.[6]

In the twentieth century, philosopher Martin Heidegger also speaks of a fourfold. His fourfold consists of the Earth, Sky, Gods, and Mortals. A context wide enough and wise enough for the mythic perspective to be reclaimed through poetic power. Again, all four interconnect to form a viable world.[7]

The Fourfold I am exploring — (a) love or loving kindness, (b) compassion, (c) joy, and (d) peace (or equanimity, as it is named in the Buddhist tradition) — is far older than Heidegger and Blake, perhaps as old as some of the native peoples. It arises in ancient India, the matrix of world religions, where it is known by two titles: the Four Divine Modes of Dwelling (or the Four

Abodes) and the Four Immeasurable Minds. Let us look at these designations more carefully.

First, these four ways of being and doing are called *divine dwellings*. When a Hindu Brahman came to the Buddha and asked what he must do to live with Brahma ("Brahma" being the name of God in his tradition), the Buddha is said to have answered: "Practice the four Brahmaviharas" (*Brahma* meaning "divine"; and *viharas*, "dwellings"). Practice the Four Divine Dwellings. Thus, these ways of dwelling open us to the divine dimension. And as we explore them and allow them to take root in us, we notice something else. We see that each is limitless.[8] Each is beyond measure. Each is open to "the more and ever more."[9] There is no end to love or compassion, or joy or peace. Practicing them is enacting the goal (already present in seed) and also taking steps that are congruent with the goal, namely acting lovingly, compassionately, joyfully, and peacefully.

The Buddha recommended that this Hindu gentleman practice a fourfold way of dwelling already present in his Hindu root tradition. What a beautiful moment! Here we uncover a teaching older than the historical Buddha — a transreligious treasure, ancient enough to have deep roots, basic enough to be found in all wisdom traditions. And, because the four are seen as mutually modifying one another, they help us to break the spell of separateness. They help us to reimagine life as profoundly interconnected. To feel the resonance with many traditions, let one of the traditions speak. "By their fruits you shall know them," says the young rabbi from Nazareth.[10] And elsewhere it is written: "What the Spirit produces is love, joy, peace, patience, kindness, goodness, faithfulness, gentleness, self-control."[11] Love, joy, and peace show up explicitly, and adding "compassion" — so dear to the Buddhist tradition — is hardly a stretch.[12] So we have assurance we are on to something central, so central that it is a touchstone of healthy and holy living.

Love, Compassion, Joy, and Peace

Let us clarify these four realities in two ways: First, *lessons from language* will help us stay flexible in the way we name the four powers. Second, *lessons by contrast* will help us to clarify the four by noting their opposites and what are called their "near enemies."

Lessons from Language

As *nouns* (as in the listing above), the four appear as qualities of character, capacities, and dispositions. There are twin dangers here: We may see them as static, unchanging, and fixed. We may see them as qualities that only individuals possess. In fact, they are dynamic realities — and they manifest at interpersonal, institutional, and planetary levels.

As *verbs*, the four are tasks or missions:

- to love — that is, to practice loving kindness or, alternately, to seek the well-being of the relationship and those within it,
- to acknowledge suffering and alleviate it,
- to receive life as gift and — being grateful — to rejoice in it, and
- to be at peace and to promote peace.

As *adverbs*, the four accompany and modify all we do, reminding us to do whatever we do (1) lovingly, (2) compassionately, (3) joyfully, and (4) peacefully.

As *modifying one another*, the four remind us that all features are present whenever any one of them is present. Because the four mutually modify one another, they are a simple yet profound introduction to a key feature of the new ecological age — namely, interconnection, interdependence, interbeing.

Lessons by Contrast

We can sharpen still further our understanding of the Fourfold Path by focusing briefly on the opposites of these four powers and on what is called, in the Buddhist tradition, their "near enemies." The near enemies are clever counterfeits, close enough to cause the unsuspecting to accept the close facsimile for the real thing.[13]

Consider the opposite of love as greed.[14] Greed wishes to take — at the expense of others. Love seeks to give — for the well-being of others. The near enemy of love is possessiveness.

Consider the opposite of compassion as hate. Hate seeks to have others suffer. Compassion seeks to be sensitive to suffering, to reduce suffering when we can, to bear suffering together when we must. The near enemy of compassion is pity.

Think of the opposite of joy as a sorrow that moves to despair — to a place where trust and hope in the meaningfulness of life fade away, and we are left as if dead. The near enemy of joy — especially being able to take joy in the good of another — is comparison.[15]

Think of the opposite of "being at peace and fostering peace" as a state of deep opposition issuing in violence, injustice, and exploitation. The near enemy of equanimity — what I am calling being at peace and promoting peace — is indifference.

These opposites are all ultimately anti-life; whereas, the four aspects of wholeness support life.

The Fourfold Path in a Context for Our Times

Because the Fourfold Path emphasizes *interconnection*, it addresses urgent needs of the new Ecological Age,[16] inviting us to expand our field of practice in an ever-widening, multilayered circle.[17]

First, we expand our hearts to include all peoples as our brothers and sisters. And as our Human-to-Human relationships broaden and deepen, we find ourselves invited:

- to stand with the prophets of every age for justice among peoples,
- to recognize that "All people are my brothers and sisters,"[18] and
- to realize that we live in them, and they live in us.

With the Roman playwright Terence we can affirm: "I am a human being and nothing human is alien to me."[19]

Second, we expand our hearts — beyond humans only — to include all beings that co-inhabit this planet with us. What is being enlarged and expanded here is the sphere of "Human-to-the-Natural-World" relationships where we are invited:

- to regard all things as our companions;
- to view the Great Family of all beings as our extended family;
- to find our place in a communion of all our kin — humans, animals, plants, minerals; and,
- to realize that we live in them and they live in us.

In the past, we were much more attuned to the natural world; we knew in our bones that all things were and are our companions. St. Francis of Assisi praised Brother Sun, Sister Moon, Brothers Wind and Air, Sister Water, Brother Fire, Mother Earth — even Sister Death.[20] Francis expands the sense of family to include the Great Family of all creatures great and small.[21]

As we expand the spheres of our relationships — both "Human-to-Human" and "Human-to-the-Natural-World" — how we relate to this enlarged circle of beings changes subtly. In Thomas Berry's words, we view the beings no longer as "a collection of objects," but rather "a communion of subjects."[22] This means we care for all we meet and that we listen to and learn from them as well. They are in us and we in them.

Third, we expand our temporal horizon to include the beings of the three times — past, present, and future. In doing so, we respond to an invitation:

- to find our place in the greater community that spans generations — a communion of the living, the dead, and the yet-to-be-born, and
- to realize that the ancestors, contemporaries, and children-yet-to-be-born live in us and we in them.

The Navajo remind us that we stand in the midst of seven generations: between the ancestors and the children yet-to-be-born — of all species. Before we act, the Navajo advise us to ask two questions: "Will this honor the ancestors? Will it serve the children?"

This opens a transgenerational context — the community of the living and the dead and those yet-to-be. One artist sees this community as a Cosmic Fish swimming through the universe, with every scale, a face.[23] Christian mystics speak of "the Communion of Saints." Suppose we expand this to include all life forms over eons of time — all holy. The ancestors, the contemporaries, and all those yet to be — of all species.[24] We are in them and they in us.

Consider the much-loved poem of Edwin Markham:

> *He drew a circle to keep me out*
> *Rebel, heretic, a thing to flout.*
> *Love and I had the wit to win*
> *We drew a circle that took him in.*[25]

So the context for working with the Fourfold Path is an ever-widening one, until we include the Circle of all Life, our deep Self, and our Mysterious Source.

An Intertwined Practice

A friend and I were talking. She was distressed because of recent conflicts between her son and his father. Finally, she said to me, "All I know to do is to increase my love."

This is our clue. In following the Fourfold Path we are increasing our love, increasing our compassion, increasing our joy, and increasing our peaceful presence. Surely in doing so, we are on solid ground, contributing to community at every level.

In difficult times, we need a middle way — between fight and flight.[26] Returning over and over to the Fourfold Path provides that middle way.

We are called to hold to what increases love and compassion, joy and peace, but to do so *without becoming oppositional*. This puts the energy of fighting into greater service. We are called to release from roles and beliefs that are "too small to live in," but to do so *without fleeing the world as our precious home*. This transforms the energy of flight to greater service.

So the invitation is to expand the circle, return to the root of the root of everything and engage in the Fourfold Path. This book is an invitation to explore that path more deeply and to live that path more fully. When we work at the roots, we nurture soul and spirit. When the roots become the branches, all benefit. The insights become practices and the practices bear good fruit. So, as we move through these chapters, let us do so in the spirit of the poet and mystic, Rumi, taking to heart his invitation:

Come, return to the root of the root of your Self.

Chapter 1

The Pathway of Love

Be of love (a little) more careful than of everything.[27]
—e. e. cummings

Beginning with Love or Loving Kindness

The first path to wholeness is love or loving kindness.[28] How
wonderful to begin with love as kindness. The Dalai Lama has said:
"My religion is kindness." Simple and profound. If I think of love
as loving kindness, then I increase my love by increasing my loving
kindness. Doing acts of kindness in a kind manner. Does that not
presence love?

In a romance language like Italian, one way to say "I love you"
is to say "Ti voglio bene." This is to say that I wish you well. I wish
good things for you. I commit to your well-being.

This form of language reminds us that love is a giving more
than a receiving. The first impulse of love is to serve the other, to
forward the other's good. In order to love in this sense, I must make
the equivalent of a Copernican Revolution: *from* no longer seeing
the other as a supporting player in my drama *to* seeing the other

as the main player in a story that is larger than both of us and in which both of us share.

Let us modify an old Hindu saying[29] in the following fashion:

> *When I do not know who you are, I manipulate you.*
> I am willing to use you to fulfill my wants and needs, without regard for you as a person in your own right. I do not see you deeply nor do I see myself deeply. I fail to honor what joins us together.

> *When I begin to know who you are, I serve you.*
> This is a service without servility as I come to see how deeply we are intertwined and how joyful I am when I am of true service to the Circle of Life, the Source, and my own deepest Self.

> *When I know more fully who you are, I am you.*
> Perhaps better than "I am you," we might say: We are "not one, not two" and through us shines always the Great Mystery.

We all begin in a pre-Copernican state. We think of ourselves as the center of the universe. Others exist to serve us. I recall a fleeting sense of myself at two or three years old. At that age, in those moments, I lived what I now call the Ego Chant: (1) Me, (2) Me want it, (3) Me want it now, (4) Me want it now, regardless. (Imagine pounding your fist in air while reciting this chant. End by stamping your feet as in a temper tantrum. This will give you the idea!) Naked ego unadorned. Too early for a real sense of the other. And, having been age two or three, we can regress to this state in an instant!

When I do not know who you are, I manipulate you. In the Ego Chant world, instead of treating you as I would wish to be treated, I treat you as a thing to be used by me, without regard for your intelligence and free will.[30] I treat you as less than a person. No one who understands what it is to be a person could agree to be treated as less than who they are. Thus, manipulation is not reversible, not reciprocal. It violates Golden Rule fairness. It is contrary to love.[31]

When I was little, I thought that, if I liked puppies, everyone would like puppies. As I grew, I learned to take on the point of view of the other. I learned to listen, to appreciate differences. Seeking the good of the other is not to be done unilaterally (as in, I know what is best for you!). In truth, often I do not know. Even my partner or friend may not know what is best for him or her. Yet in the spirit of inquiring together, we can be present for each other. We can come to understand more fully what is good for thee and me and we. We can seek each other's good in the context of our relationship and all it serves.

When I know more fully who you are, I serve you. To understand this beyond codependence requires another breakthrough. We must break through a see-saw world of separate selves, wherein if I am up, you must be down, and if I am down, you must be up. Here the best we can hope for is "win-win." Yet love goes beyond "win-win," beyond the whole world of separateness. Love shows us how deeply we are already and always interconnected.

James Edwin Loder speaks of love as "the non-possessive delight in the particularity of the other."[32] He is describing a love between grown-ups, between those who work to reverse the Ego Chant. He is pointing to a world where persons are recognized as centers in their own life, not simply means to satisfy my wants or needs. For love to increase, certain tendencies in me must decrease. I must break out of my self-enclosure if I am to meet you as the holy particular you are and explore the holy possibilities that we might be.

Scott Peck took the risk of giving a definition of love in his 1978 classic, *The Road Less Traveled*.[33] Love, he said is "the will to extend one's self for the purpose of nurturing one's own or another's spiritual growth." Here "well-being" becomes "spiritual growth." Growth adds the notion that we can become better at nurturing our own or another's good. Spiritual growth places the process in a wisdom narrative. And the emphasis is on love as an action rather than simply a feeling.[34] An action requiring will and commitment to the well-being of the relationship, the parties within it, and all it serves. In mature love, consistency and character matter. And, love is ever in process. As one sage wrote: "Life is not a finished action; love is not a completed thought."[35] Love unfolds in ever-surprising ways and requires many mindful practices. Yet Scott Peck is right to see love as a verb, to see loving as giving. To love we must go out from our self-enclosure and contribute beyond ourselves.

Beyond the world of separateness, we encounter a more excellent way.[36] We notice that my well-being and your well-being are not so separate. I can take joy in your happiness and you can take joy in mine. We may even begin to perceive a third reality — the subtle field of the relationship itself — like a garden in which we are growing. Without any servility, we can "Think partnership

first and then you and me." We are "holons" in Arthur Koestler's term, wholes within ourselves and parts of larger wholes, as cells are part of organs which are parts of bodies which form relational fields of varying sizes: friendships, family and work relationships, through organizations of all sorts up to the planet itself as a whole within the still larger context of the universe unfolding.

Interlude: Three Names for Love

In the West, we have three Greek names for love: *eros, philia,* and *agape*.[37]

I think of eros as the primal power of attraction at work in all things from atoms and molecules, through all the forms of life, especially those species who invented or perpetuated sex.[38] The mysteries of sex, like nature itself, can be gentle as a caress and wild as a hurricane.

Plato relates a tale told by his mentor Socrates. But Socrates gives credit to this teaching about eros to a woman, Diotima. Diotima taught him that the all-pervading nature of attraction follows us — the embodied ones — throughout our lives. As new horizons open for us, so eros like a shapeshifter follows us. We experience eros first in attraction to bodies and physical beauty, then (without negating the former) adding attraction to beautiful souls, next attraction to learning and the arts, and then in a moment of insight to glimpse the source of eros in its triple guise: the true, the good, and the beautiful. The source of eros is partly present in everything. Eros is that longing in us for the true, the good, and the beautiful. And these three are not separate, but inter-be. Such is the lovely hymn to eros Socrates shares. A view of the erotic that blessedly never leaves us. And we come to understand that, in seeking the true and good and beautiful anywhere, we are seeking fullness, seeking wholeness. Even when we go astray, Aquinas will later say, we are still seeking what we believe to be good.

The second name for love is philia — the love of friendship.[39] Philia stands between eros and agape. It is central in more ways than one. Here is my variation of a Lakota prayer:

> I join my breath to your breath,
> that we may be
> committed to our own and each other's growing,
> committed to our partnerships and all they serve,
> that we may finish our road together.

Our friendship is a greater third, as if the glass bowl of "who I am" and the glass bowl of "who you are" are both floating in a much vaster bowl. Present are (1) your growth and deepening, (2) my growth and deepening, and (3) the growth and deepening of our relationship.

When I am aware of myself and yourself and what joins us, then dialogue is possible, feedback is possible, growth in sensitivity is possible.

When my daughter Heather was a little girl, I took her to see a play. Afterwards, I asked her what she thought of plays as compared to movies. "The thing about plays," she said, "is when you look at the people, they look back." The thing about friendships is when you look at your friend, your friend looks back. When you speak and listen to your friend, your friend is able to listen and to speak to you. Each of you is concerned for the other's good and for the good of the relational field that you share and co-create. With caring feedback, skillfully given and received, we each learn more about our shadow side, our stuck points, our emotional patterns. Perhaps we find, outside of our family of origin, what psychoanalyst Alice Miller calls "enlightened witnesses." Then new healing can occur. In such a friendship, we can speak and listen, see and be seen, know and be known in new ways that allow us possibilities we had not seen before. Such friendships also permit us to return to *loving-as-giving* in healthy rather than unhealthy ways. American psychologist James Mark Baldwin once remarked that every genuine act of self-sacrifice is also an act of self-enhancement. I would add that the self ("little self") that is sacrificed is not the same as the self ("larger self") that is enhanced.

The Buddhist therapist, David Brazier, sees love as the antidote to greed. Brazier writes: "Love heals greed, as compassion heals hate. In greed, I want to get things for myself, to incorporate everything into me and my orbit. In love, I want to give to others, to respect things just as they are, unconditionally. In . . . comparison with humanistic psychology . . . , just as compassion is close to empathy, love is close to positive regard."[40]

The third name of love is agape. It is commonly defined as unconditional love. And it is said that this is the way God loves. Agape is how God loves us and all our brothers and sisters, all our kin.

First, this is not the picture of God that many of us were taught. We were taught that God's love was conditioned on our thoughts, words, and deeds. Such a "God" appeared in a world of reward and punishment.

Yet, to adapt a thought of Rumi, "There is a field beyond reward and punishment, beyond praise and blame. Let's meet there." In that field we come to know that we have always been loved. And we glimpse such love when humans act in accord with their highest and deepest Self.

- A mother tells her estranged son, "I love you no matter what. You are my son and nothing will stop me from loving you. You can receive that love or not, but know it is there and will be there whenever you choose to accept it."

- A wife takes her bandages off after a mastectomy. She is looking at herself naked in the mirror for the first time since the surgery. Her husband has asked to be with her. He says to her: "You are beautiful and nothing essential about you has changed."

- Nelson Mandela emerges from 27 years in prison and forgives his captors.

- In Archbishop Desmond Tutu's presence, the South African Truth and Reconciliation Commission creates conditions where bitter enemies face what they have done and make new starts.

- The Amish in Lancaster County, Pennsylvania, find a way to care for the families of five slain schoolgirls and the family of the one who perpetrated the attack before taking his own life.

- There are even times when God is forgiven, as in the story of the Jews in the death camps who put God on trial, condemned him, and then went on to perform the ritual prayers of the Sabbath.

The Sufi saint, Rab'ia, loves with this unconditional love when she speaks to her God in this fashion: "Lord, if I worship you from fear of Hell, burn me in Hell. If I worship you from hope of heaven, exclude me from heaven. But if I worship you for your own sake alone, then come to me."[41]

Agape is to love the Whole from the Whole or even as the Whole. "That of God" in me loves "that of God" in all beings. And all is well. Our response is humility, gratitude, and generosity.[42] And more subtly, a new quality of listening to the still small voice within and to the hidden wholeness in those we meet.

So these three intertwine: eros, philia, and agape. Each seasoning the others while we live embodied and among others, "in the City and under the Mercy."[43]

Loving Kindness Meditation

In the Buddhist tradition (where we started) loving kindness accents the positive. Loving kindness meditation[44] encourages us to extend the circle of love and kindness.

1. Starting closest to home, we send loving kindness to ourselves and our loved ones, wishing all to be well, happy, free from needless suffering, wishing that we come to know who we are and rest in our true nature.

2. Then we send loving kindness to neutral persons, perhaps slight acquaintances, wishing them to be well, happy, free from needless suffering, wishing that they know who they are and rest in their true nature.

3. Step by step, we move to people we find difficult or even those we think of as enemies. We send loving kindness to them, wishing that they be well, happy, and free from needless suffering, wishing that they know who they are and rest in their true nature.

Going Forward

Each of the four paths intertwines with all of the others. We shall learn more of love as we explore compassion and joy and peace. Here I have focused on love as a verb, on love as opposed to greed,[45] on love as a giving, an action of service, an affirming of the other. I have also noted that in enhancing the other's spiritual growth we also contribute to our own and that of all our kin.

Attractions always accompany us. Happily, we are embodied beings. So eros is never far. Friendship brings in the very particular other to whom we listen, to whom we speak. Certainly justice is a condition of love.[46] Yet love goes beyond anything we "deserve." Always we have been loved beyond measure. "Fear not," we are told. Lessening fear, we can open our heart, decrease our judgments, and learn to love more fully.

In our time, genuine spirituality begins with interconnection, interbeing, interdependence. Spirituality usually echoes the narrative of one or more of the great wisdom traditions of humankind. This I find heartening, since all great wisdom traditions teach "By their fruits you will know them."[47] And the fruits of the Spirit, the fruits of a well-lived life, resonate across traditions.[48]

While lingering with the wisdom traditions, I wish to bring in perhaps the most loved of scriptural passages on love, from the letter of Paul to the young church at Corinth. I offer a slightly different variation, so that we may hear this good guidance anew:

When I truly love,

I am patient and kind.

I do not envy others, but rather rejoice in the good of others.

I am not boastful, not caught up in my own importance.

When I truly love,

I do not put on airs. I am not rude.

I recognize that humility and courtesy are marks of love.

When I truly love,

I do not insist on my way.

I do not become angry.

I do not rejoice over injustice, I stand gently with truth.

When I truly love,

I never give up, never lose faith.

I am always hopeful and endure all things.

Such love, I find, does not fail. [49]

This sentiment echoes even in the words of a five-year-old girl. The story is this:

> The family consists of a mother (an artist and teacher) and her two daughters, Stella, age 5, and Sophie, age 10. Each week, the family would write a "saying of the week" on a large piece of art paper. They would then hang the saying in a prominent place in their house as a reminder.
>
> For some years, the family has been suffering the pain that comes with the dissolution of a marriage. One week, the younger daughter said: "Mommy, write: We won't give up on love." Good advice when one has hope for love reconciled. Yet even if the love will not return as it once was, still good advice: "Mommy, write: We won't give up on love."

This is the first path — one that goes on and on. The challenge is ever to increase our love. To see the Whole and each particular more clearly. To love each creature and event that comes to us more dearly, and to follow the way more nearly — day by day.[50]

Surely, for the sake of all the children, we will heed the words of Stella. We will not give up on love.

Chapter 2

The Pathway of Compassion

On and on the rain will fall
  like tears from a star,
  like tears from a star.

On and on the rain will say
  how fragile we are
  how fragile we are.[51]

—Sting

In the Fourfold Path to Wholeness, we glimpse four mysterious "pointers to the Great Mystery." They are *love, compassion, joy,* and *peace*. Four dancers dancing one dance. "How can we know the dancer from the dance?" W. B. Yeats asks.[52] "At the still point, there the dance is . . . and there is only the dance," T. S. Eliot responds.[53] So if we wish to come to life more fully in every moment, wisdom suggests we cultivate these four: love and compassion, joy and peace.

As we explore compassion, let us also keep in mind the other three of the quartet, noting especially, at this juncture, how love and compassion intertwine.

The Pathway of Compassion

We were teaching together, my wife Gregg and I, doing a retreat with young ministers in the North Carolina mountains. Gregg said: "Do you not know you are wounded miracles?"[54] This, for me, opens the door to what is distinctive about compassion. The fact that we are wounded points to suffering and the release from suffering. The fact that we are miracles provides a larger context. The fact that we are both wounded and miracles bonds us together — with our Source, our deepest Self, and with all who companion us on the way.

Two Sides of Life: A Teaching Story

> Once upon a time, in a place both far and near, a young prince was born. From the beginning, the marks of greatness were upon him, and all realized that he would either become a great ruler or a great sage. The boy's father wanted his son to follow him as a great ruler, so he devised a plan. "As my son grows," the father thought, "he will desire what young men desire: wine, women, and song." So the father provided his son with such pleasures in full measure: beautiful women, fine food, entertainment fit for a king. One thing alone was

forbidden: The son was not allowed to venture outside the vast precincts of the palace.

The prince reached adulthood, married, and had a son. Yet, more and more, the forbidden territory beyond the palace beckoned him. One day a mysterious charioteer appeared and offered to take the prince outside. So it was. Out beyond the palace walls they traveled. On the outside, the prince encountered a *sick person*, an *old person*, a *dead person*, and, somewhat later, a *sage* in monk's robes.

Now everything changed. The prince confronted two sides of life: Not only health but sickness. Not only youth but age. Not only life but death. How, he asked himself, can I live in awareness of both sides of existence? Perhaps the answer lay along the path of the sage. And so he entered the way of the forest dweller, the way of the ascetic.

In his palace life, the prince experienced the path of self-fulfillment. Eventually, he found it wanting, for it failed to address human suffering. In his life as an ascetic, the prince followed the way of self-denial. Eventually, he found this unsatisfactory as well. He noticed that repressing aspects of life only brought them forth more vividly. At this juncture, the prince vowed to meditate with fierce determination until he could find a middle way between the way of self-fulfillment and the way of self-denial. Coming to a world-shattering realization, the prince — Gotama Siddhartha by name — woke up. Since then, he has been called the Buddha, which simply means "the one who woke up."[55]

"I teach two things:" the Buddha said, "there is suffering and there is release from suffering." The second of the four paths to wholeness aids us to face suffering, to understand it, to transform what we can, to bear what we must. We call this second way of dwelling *"compassion."*[56] Compassion begins with empathy — the ability to stand with others and see through their eyes the contours of their world. In a fuller sense, compassion shows us how to be in a world that brings us both suffering and also moments beyond suffering, moments of happiness and joy. Let us return to what the future Buddha encountered:

- a sick person,
- an old person, and
- a dead person.

That person is me. I am a person who can get sick and does get sick. I am a person who can age and does age. I am a person who can die and will die. I am a being that can be hurt at many levels. I can suffer sickness of the body, of the mind, of the spirit. I will age and with age find myself struggling with such issues as loneliness, helplessness, and despair. And I will die. So will all of my fellow creatures.

In the Buddha's time, a young mother watched as her baby son became ill and died. Devastated with grief, she went to the Buddha with her baby's lifeless body in her arms. She pleaded with him to revive her son. The Buddha said he would revive her son if she could bring him a mustard seed from a house untouched by death.

In going from house to house, she learned how pervasive is death. She also learned a second lesson: how curiously comforting it is to have our grief acknowledged and shared by others.

Compassion aids us to reduce the suffering we can and to bear the suffering we must.

The Roots of Suffering

Following the Buddha as our guide to compassion, we can go further. For the Buddha traced suffering back to its roots and shared these insights with us in what have come to be called the *Four Noble Truths*:

1. **There is suffering.**

   I distinguish two types of suffering: (a) "necessary suffering" and (b) "unnecessary suffering." Necessary suffering comes with the human condition and is unavoidable. We are vulnerable; we age; we die. Unnecessary suffering (or surplus suffering) is suffering that is caused by humans and can be reduced by humans. Think of wars and exploitation and all the injustices we inflict on one another and the natural world.[57]

2. **Suffering has its causes** (called the three poisons). Generically, they are:

   (a) greed, (b) hatred, and (c) ignorance, *or*

   (a) attachment, (b) aversion, and (c) confusion, *or*

   (a) clinging, (b) condemning, and (c) identifying (with less than all we are).

3. **If we reduce the causes** (the three poisons), **then we will reduce the suffering.**

4. **There is a way to do this, a spiral path having**
   (a) an insight/commitment phase,
   (b) a service or ethical phase, and
   (c) a stillness or meditative phase.[58]

The crucial teaching here is to put the diagnosis to work. To decrease greed, hate, and ignorance. To increase healing and wholeness in our speaking, acting, and living. To stop, look, and listen in a mindful, meditative spirit. When we do these things consistently, we remove the illusions that obscure our true nature. We allow our true nature — already healthy and whole — to shine forth.

Love and Compassion

Love or loving kindness and compassion belong together. In fact, they can be seen as antidotes to the first two of the three poisons, namely, greed and hatred. Zen therapist David Brazier distinguishes between them in this fashion:[59]

Love	Compassion
Seeking the good of the other, seeking the growth of the other	Sensitivity to the suffering of the other; seeking to alleviate the other's suffering
Thus, love heals greed, i.e., wanting to take from the other.	Thus, compassion heals hatred, i.e., wishing that the other suffer.

Both love and compassion require us to give up the illusion that we are at the center of the world and everything revolves around us! They prompt us to reduce our self-concern and enlarge our world. To see that there are many centers — each person a center of his or her own world — and yet all held by a common life.

Relieving the Suffering We Can: The Ethical Steps

Ethical practices help us to notice that what we say and do has consequences to us, to others, and to the relational fields in which we dwell.[60] Thus, an undergirding condition for compassion is to engage in ethical practices. I wish to link ethics with release from suffering. To do this, I offer a simplified version of the five precepts (or mindfulness trainings) from contemporary Buddhism.[61] The general format I am using is this:

Aware of the suffering caused by _____ (a gross form of a vice), *I am committed to cultivate* _____ (a corrective virtue) *and to reduce* _____ (the subtle roots of the vice) *in its many forms.*[62]

1. Aware of the suffering caused by *destruction of life,* I am committed to cultivate compassion and reverence for life and to reduce *"killing"* in its many forms.

2. Aware of the suffering caused by *stealing, social injustice, and exploitation,* I am committed to cultivate loving kindness and generosity and to reduce *"taking what is not given"* in its many forms.

3. Aware of the suffering caused by *sexual misconduct* I am committed to cultivate sexual responsibility and true intimacy and to reduce *"sexual manipulation"* in its many forms.

4. Aware of the suffering caused *by unmindful speech and the inability to listen,* I am committed to cultivate loving speech and deep listening and to reduce *"failure of communication"* in its many forms.

5. Aware of the suffering caused by unmindful consumption, I am committed to cultivate mindful eating, drinking, and consuming and to reduce *"destructive addiction"* in its many forms.[63]

When we are unmindful, when we are asleep in our life, we tend to cause all sorts of surplus suffering. When we are awake and alert and mindful of what we are saying and doing, we realize we have a choice — a choice to recognize and reduce unnecessary suffering for ourselves and all our kin.[64] These reminders call us to remember who we are at our core and what we are about together. They are needed over and over again at the interpersonal, institutional, international, and planetary levels of life.[65]

The great wisdom traditions — East and West — all provide guidance for basic conduct of a humane and liberating sort.[66] Actions have consequences; people (and other beings) have basic worth and appropriate rights. We are reminded to seek what is good for the whole and fair to each participant-part. We are helped to remember our Source, our deep Self, and all our brothers and sisters in the Circle of Life.

Bearing the Suffering We Must — The Contemplative Lessons[67]

Sitting at night with a sick child. Having done what we can, we bear what we must.

Waiting for a loved one to return home and fearing the worst. Having done what we can, we bear what we must.

Learning that someone we love has a life-threatening illness. Having done what we can, we bear what we must.

The first pole of compassion is reducing unnecessary suffering where we can. The second pole of compassion is bearing together what we cannot change. What do we learn from facing together the suffering we cannot change?

Recall my wife, Gregg, telling the young ministers: "You are wounded miracles." So are we all. This insight opens a door to compassion. Because we are miracles, the glory lies within and around us. Because we are wounded, we know what it is to be hurt by others and to hurt others. Because we are implicated in the web of suffering, contrition and forgiveness are fitting personal responses.

A contrite heart. We are humble when we know our own true size — both miraculous and wounded still. We are contrite when we realize that our words and actions are capable of creating heaven or hell in every moment.[68] Forgiveness of ourselves and others arises out of this double awareness — looking deeply and seeing how our actions and those of others can open or close our hearts, especially to the extent we are greedy, hateful, and ignorant.[69] Here forgiveness is akin to seeing ourselves and others in our surface and deep natures and in our ever-unfinished trajectories. I think of such forgiveness in the spirit of the words by a Benedictine sister, Mary Lou Kownacki: "Engrave this upon my heart: There isn't anyone you couldn't love once you've heard their story." This is not to engage in justifications. Rather it is to be stripped of justifications and stand as a beautiful, unskilled, wholly human one. This is close to what the Japanese mean by the word *"bombu"* — "a foolish creature of wayward passions."[70] Or even what the Zen master Rinzai called "true humans in the mass of raw flesh — to see them is to love them."

Deeper Learnings

> *Love, compassion, joy and peace*
> *dwell in us to our increase.*
> *Love, compassion, joy and peace*
> *say to us: release, release.*

When we have done what is ours to do, we bear together what we must. We are called to union with our Source and communion with all our kin. From our Source, we begin to notice that there is sufficiency in the graciousness of the Ever-Present Origin.[71] We are enough and have enough — in ourselves and those who companion us — to live a worthy life right here and right now. We begin to notice that we are not alone, rather we are "all-one."

We share with our fellow creatures susceptibility to suffering, to sickness, to aging, and death. Here we bear with one another. In our time we are recovering what our ancestors never forgot — that we are members of the Great Web of Life, the Great Family.[72] The entire Circle of Life is my kin. In this context, we can say:

> We do not do the Great Work of love and compassion for ourselves alone.
>
> We do not do the Great Work of love and compassion by ourselves alone.
>
> We do not do the Great Work of love and compassion by our own power alone.

All of these mantras of mine bring us back to the present moment where the Source is available and the circle of companions stretches over generations.

In the present
At the still point
Life abundant
Grateful heart.

In knowing ourselves in the light of compassion, we know ourselves as wounded miracles. We return to the Source, return to ourselves, return to all who companion us. We live and grow in the context of "interbeing."[73] Hence, love and compassion are a call to walk out of our house — our self-enclosure — and realize that we belong to the whole. In that sense, we are already home. Gratitude wells up. Humility and a contrite heart follow. Forgiveness also. Recall again the words of Edwin Markham:

He drew a circle to keep me out
Rebel, heretic, a thing to flout.
Love and I had the wit to win
We drew a circle that took him in.[74]

In compassion, we are ever drawing wider circles, until all beings are our brothers and sisters and all things our companions.[75]

Chapter 3

The Pathway of Joy

For the raindrop, joy is in entering the river.[76]
— Mirza Ghalib

Sunrise over mountains on a bright summer morning. Moonrise over oceans on a clear winter night. Those with hearts open are continually surprised by joy.[77]

"Tell them that joy is not the same as happiness." The voice is my wife's, and the distinction is one she has long utilized in teaching and counseling.[78] The distinction is this: Happiness is dependent on circumstances; joy is not. My wife Gregg's image is a bowl. For her, events are like items — or small packages — in the bowl. Life is the bowl itself, hence not identified with the contents of the bowl. I fully agree.[79]

Let us look more closely at this way of proceeding. Here, "happiness" is dependent on circumstances. As the song says: "Sometimes I'm happy. Sometimes I'm blue. My disposition depends on you."[80] The incidents come and go. So do our commentaries and emotional reactions. Joy, as I am using the term, is deeper. Joy comes from a place where we realize we are already connected to the Whole.[81] With practice, we can evoke joy even in the midst of sadness. We do this in at least three ways:[82]

- By seeing life as richer than stories, we let go of judgments and negative emotions. Freedom arises; we come home to joy.

- By seeing life as gift and allowing gratitude, gratefulness or great fullness, to emerge, we realize that, in ourselves and those who companion us, we have all we need to live a life of quality right here and right now.

- By seeing life as creative and endlessly capable of surprising us, we smile and, with the smile, joy appears as well, humanizing our imperfect perfection.

Ghalib writes, "For the raindrop, joy is in entering the river."[83] Yet perhaps that too is an incident, an occasion. Perhaps joy resides still further down — in the depth dimension of the ocean, in the place to which all rivers flow, a place where we mirror the whole — in union and communion, all at once. Ghalib may well be pointing to the same thing, seeing joy as arising from the depth dimension of life, a reunion with the Whole, a homecoming.

The raindrop descends, releasing from the cloud, heading for the river. We follow the raindrop by releasing from the surface occasions and our commentaries on them. Releasing our story-driven judgments, releasing our emotional reactions, evoking gratitude, returning gratefully to what is. Then "deep calls to deep."[84] Then joy is found to have been there all along, awaiting the invitation to manifest in things both great and small.

I am exploring four dimensions of dwelling in wholeness. All four aspects are present in each moment. Hence, joy arrives with three companions: (1) love (or loving kindness), (2) compassion (arising from an awareness of how fragile we are), and (3) a sense of peace and equanimity. Joy arrives, we might say, lovingly, compassionately, and peacefully. In fact, as we shall see, the way to joy is indirect. Imagine practicing joy grimly! The reality is far simpler.

"We all have within us a center of stillness surrounded by silence." So spoke Dag Hammarskjöld in dedicating the meditation room at the United Nations Headquarters in New York City.[85] I experience joy connected to that stillness, joy as a quality of that silence. Joy has different colors, different moods — sometimes exuberant and liberating, sometimes quiet and content. Always available. We already have all we seek. That is the secret of secrets. Joy, born of gratitude, is the affective dimension of that realization.

> Returning to stillness
> Basking in silence
> Gratefulness rising
> Joyful the day.

Celtic mythology tells of a pool surrounded by purple hazelnut trees — deep in a mysterious forest. The hazelnuts drop gently into the pool. The salmon — the Celtic wisdom fish — come to the surface to feed. Nourishment descends effortlessly. Wisdom arises effortlessly. In a mythic way of understanding, the wisdom pool lies before us and within us — in the heart of all. That center point is a threshold where the two worlds meet. Ever-present, yet veiled — until the veil lifts, until the mists clear. Every moment, touching stillness. Every place, touching center. Such a pool — deep within us — provides us living water. Such a pool unites the Great Mystery, my never-fully-known Self, and the equally mysterious Circle of all Life. The spirit of the pool is suggested by a smile.

This Celtic image suggests three aspects of joy, all to be unfolded as we go.

- Joy as linked to releasing. When the hazelnuts release, the salmon arise. When we release our identification with thoughts and emotions, roles and fixed ideas, then for a time we are free and joy wells up.

- Joy as grounded in gratefulness. The salmon and all that is — these are present as pure gift, beyond anything deserved, simply given. When this is recognized and we choose to live from this awareness, then joy arises from gratefulness, as thanks, prayer, and praise.

- Joy as linked to a smile of the heart — bringing humility and gentle humor to all we do. As if the whole — the pond and the hazelnut trees and the salmon — all exist within the feeling tone of the great heart of us all. A heart that smiles and blesses.[86]

In some moments, we glimpse the beauty of the Whole in every part. Then, every moment can be a joyful receiving, a joyful releasing, and a joyful remembering of life as gift, life as grace. Here is the power of distinguishing joy and happiness. We see that joy partakes of the unconditional, the ever-surprising, the unlimited. As the gospel singer Shirley Caesar says: "This joy I have — the world didn't give it, the world can't take it away."[87]

1. Love as agape reaches to the unconditional — to love "no matter what" — to love throughout a life — for richer and poorer, in sickness and in health.

2. Compassion reaches to the unconditional. I think of the gentle monk Ryōkan, Japan's counterpart to St. Francis of Assisi, who writes:

> Oh that my monk's robes
> Were wide enough
> To gather up all
> The suffering people
> In this floating world.[88]

Terrible are the harms we do and terrible the harms we suffer. Yet some among us can forgive beyond any bounds we set for forgiveness. In so doing, they remove the last suffering from ourselves and others. They show an unconditional compassion. No enemies, only the "wounded miracles" that we continue to be.[89]

3. Joy also reaches the unconditional, arising from a place not dependent on conditions — from the bowl of life itself, not the

events that are in the bowl. If we have eyes to see and heart to feel, this joy — born of gratefulness for the sheer gift of life and all it contains — can shine through, even on the worst of days.

A Startling Discovery

Joy lives in a world beyond reward and punishment, beyond praise and blame. Deep joy is ever available — not by making it happen but by clearing the way for it to appear. As a road goes on and on, so the joy appears as "More and ever more."[90] No wonder that Meister Eckhart called it Wandering Joy.[91] The joy is ever deepening as we walk in mindfulness open to the mystery. The joy, like the love and the compassion, is from God and of God and towards God.[92] No wonder the Jesuit scientist and mystic Pierre Teilhard de Chardin could say: "Joy is the most infallible sign of the presence of God."

Joy and a Smile

The verb form of joy is to rejoice, to enjoy.[93] Rejoice always — a theme in many scriptures. Zen Master Thich Nhat Hanh tells us: "Sometimes your joy is the source of your smile, but sometimes your smile can be the source of your joy." One of his themes is to enjoy one's practice, whether mindful sitting or walking or whatever else we are doing.

> Breathing in, I calm my body.
> Breathing out, I smile.
> Dwelling in the present moment
> I know this is a wonderful moment.[94]

Smiling, besides a great relaxation, is also a practice of joy. Enjoy your practice.

A wife made a request of her husband, asking him to do a task. He started to set about it, but she stopped him. "One of the conditions of satisfaction for my request," she added, "is that you do the task happily, joyfully, wholeheartedly, not with a grim and grudging spirit." Joy here appears as an adverb, modifying and shifting the feeling tone of whatever is being done.

Joy and Gratefulness

Joy has its roots in gratitude, gratefulness, great fullness. Here, we can do no better than take as our guide the wise Benedictine monk, David Steindl-Rast.[95] Gratitude is a practice for invoking joy. As we grow in gratitude, our joy grows too. If we could be grateful for every moment, seeing all as gift, then would not our joy be unbounded?

Brother David has a mantra of sorts: "In daily life, we must see that it is not happiness that makes us grateful, but gratefulness that makes us happy."[96] I would rephrase as: "In daily life, it is not joy that makes us grateful, but gratefulness that brings us to joy." Recall again the analogy of life as the bowl and events as circumstances within the bowl. Gratitude begins with the fact that we are not owed life — it is a gift. We do not deserve the life we live. It comes to us gratis. Not owed, not earned, not deserved. Life is given and gift, if we choose to so see it. Breathing in life as gift, we learn to breathe out gratefulness.

What I am calling the Whole or Great Mystery, Brother David speaks of as "the More and ever more."[97] Suppose we think of joy as an aspect of "the More and ever more." Then, any time we touch the real with love, compassion, and peace, we are apt to be surprised by joy. As I have said, such joy appears in many modes — from quiet contentment to ecstasy and abiding bliss.[98] All deserve respect.

We are beginning to see that joy, at its depth, is unconditional, independent of circumstances or conditions. So also are great love and great compassion. So also deep inner peace or equanimity. All proceed from the deepest core of our being which has many names and no name.[99] Once again, the secret of secrets — that we already have all we seek, that the union/communion is within and surrounding us at every moment. A sign in a local coffee shop says: "There is always, always, always something to be grateful for." Grateful for what we are receiving, we give thanks. Giving thanks, we evoke joy.

Furthermore gratefulness/great fullness points us to the spaciousness and specialness of the whole and each participant. William Blake reminds us:

> To see the world in a grain of sand
> And a heaven in a wild flower
> Hold infinity in the palm of your hand
> and eternity in an hour.[100]

This echoes an Eastern theme. *Sunyata* is the spaciousness of all things, empty of fixity, open to all possibilities. *Tathata* is the particularity of each thing, uniquely itself and uniquely mirroring the whole from a particular point of view. Joy flourishes when we encounter all that is with new eyes and a new heart — open to the spaciousness and specialness of each being.

A Test Case: Sympathetic Joy

The third mode of dwelling is often called sympathetic joy, that is, the capacity to take joy in the success or achievements of another. For many, this is a test case — something many believe is difficult to do. Why should this be so? Surely if I love you, I wish you well and desire your good. Indeed, a prime example of taking joy in the success of another is rejoicing in the success of my children.[101] When this does occur, it may be that I see my children as part of myself in ways I do not see a colleague. If I broke the spell of separateness and saw all beings as my brothers and sisters, then perhaps I would experience their success as enhancing my own. At some deep level, I would realize how deeply we are intertwined.

What stops me from rejoicing in the success of, say, a colleague or neighbor? Our first clue is noticing that we are entering the realm of comparison. In the tradition, comparison is called the near enemy of joy, meaning it is a close facsimile. Close enough to confuse us but not to enlighten us. Once comparison infects us, it suggests "life as a see-saw." If you are up, I must be down — and vice versa. At the core of this is the first falsehood — that life is insufficient, that there is not enough praise to go around. The second falsehood is that we

are radically separate. One remedy here is to go beyond (a) the superiority complex, (b) the inferiority complex, and (c) the equality
complex![102] Reduce envy and jealousy. Envy is a form of greed — I
want what the other has or seems to have. Jealousy is a form of hate
— I do not want you to have what I have. I want to diminish you
in certain ways.[103] Reducing envy and jealousy, we die to a smaller
sense of self and rise to a larger-minded sense of our interconnection
with all.

Joy and Autumn Simplicity

Letting go is also a way to joy. Letting go of disempowering
stories and constrictive, oppositional emotions.[104] This returns us to
nature, to simple gifts, to the mystery of what is — at surface and
midpoint and depth.[105] And in freedom, we experience joy.

I am reminded of the dictum of the Third Zen patriarch Seng-
Ts'an: "Do not seek for the truth (or reality). Only stop having
opinions."[106] This is the way of dis-identification, as in this exercise:

I have a body,
    and thoughts about my body. Plus likes and dislikes about
    my body.

I have a body. I am not my body only.

> I am a center of consciousness. A unique reflection of the Great Mystery of all that is.

I have emotions,

> and thoughts about these emotions. Plus likes and dislikes about my emotions.

I have emotions. I am not my emotions only.

> I am a center of consciousness. A unique reflection of the Great Mystery of all that is.

I have roles,

> and thoughts about my roles. Plus likes and dislikes around my roles.

I have roles. I am not my roles only.

> I am a center of consciousness. A unique reflection of the Great Mystery of all that is.

I have beliefs,

> and thoughts about my beliefs. Plus likes and dislikes generated by my beliefs.

I have beliefs. I am not my beliefs only.

> I am a center of consciousness. A unique reflection of the Great Mystery of all that is.[107]

In all of the great traditions, there is a time when discursive thoughts get in the way of our deepening. Yet we fear that loosening our identification with our thoughts and emotions, roles and rules, ideas and ideologies will cast us into confusion and we will lose our way. Here context is everything — a context including healthy norms that allow love and compassion, joy and peace, to flourish. By their fruits you shall know them, and the fruits of the spirit are always love and compassion (which includes a sense of justice and mercy), joy, and peace. So letting go of small-minded views does not diminish us. It opens us to the mystery within us and between and among us. It widens the circle.

Joy and the Winter Sage

Becoming a sage is not taking on a new role, as if sagehood were all about me! Becoming a sage is more like letting God be God through a disappearing "me." I become a mirror or, better, a window. I become a place where my being and acting are more and more in union with the Great Mystery. More and more for the sake of all my kin. Empty of self, the dazzling suchness of life appears.

What is present mirrors Source, Self, and Circle of All Life in non-possessive love and compassion, joy and peace.

Hear now the words of the fourteenth-century North Indian mystic, Lalla:

> The soul, like the moon,
> is new, and always new again.
> Continuously creating.
>
> Since I scoured my mind
> and my body, I too, Lalla,
> Am new, each moment.
>
> My teacher told me one thing,
> Live in the soul.
> When that was so
> I began to go naked
> and dance.[108]

Chapter 4

The Pathway of Peace

Suddenly, a great stillness arises within you,
an unfathomable sense of peace.
And within that peace, there is a great joy.
And within that joy, there is love.
And at the innermost core, there is the sacred,
the immeasurable,
That which cannot be named.[109]

—Eckhart Tolle

The Fourfold Path to Wholeness aids us to live and act more lovingly, more compassionately, more joyfully, and more peacefully. In this chapter, we explore equanimity, by which I mean "being at peace and being a presence for peace."

Here is the first of two stories:

> Evening in Los Angeles. A middle-aged African American man scanned the restaurant looking for his friends. Tall with athletic build, he moved with an air of calm authority. Not finding his friends, the man decided to wait in the restaurant bar. As he started to sit down at the bar, another man,

arriving at the same time, turned and said: "You're sitting in my seat!" And after a slight pause, the new arrival continued. "Just like *you* people!" The black man paused a moment and said, in a voice somehow both courteous and compassionate, "What is happening with you?" The other — as if stopped in his tracks — responded: "My wife just left me."

The African American who turned away wrath with compassion was Larry Ward, a meditation teacher in the tradition of Thich Nhat Hanh. Larry told the story at a retreat he was leading in North Carolina some years later. "This," he said, "is the fruit of practice." Larry told a second story during that retreat:

He was in China in the entourage of Thich Nhat Hanh (or Thây — pronounced "tie" — meaning "teacher" — as he is affectionately called). They were in the Chinese hinterlands where the Zen master had been invited to bless the re-opening of an ancient monastery. Restaurants of any size were few. Only one nearby restaurant could accommodate the party. As the group entered, they noticed, high on the walls around the central eating area, cages with various animals in them. When someone ordered, the cooks would take the chosen animal, slaughter it, and prepare it to be eaten. The people in Thây's party were mainly Buddhist monks and nuns, and, as such, vegetarians. The sight of animals ready to be butchered for their meal produced much discomfort among them. However, Thây walked with no perturbation whatsoever. As he and the group had their vegetarian fare, he ate as mindfully as if in his home monastery. At the end of the meal, he asked the restaurant owner, "Is it permissible to purchase some of the animals and release them?" It was indeed permissible and so it was done. Larry Ward again said: "This is the fruit of practice."

What do these two incidents have to teach us about equanimity — about the practice of inner and outer peace? In both instances, reactivity arose or could have arisen. To react is to have no space between incoming stimulus and outgoing response.[110] In the first case, a racist remark was a possible trigger. In the second, a commitment to the well-being of animals was a possible trigger. Our dislikes (fears and challenges) and our likes (commitments and values) can both trigger reactivity.

The key to less reactivity is on the sign posted by railroad crossings: "Stop, look, and listen!" First you must stop, pause, and interrupt the soap opera of your restless mind. Then you can realize

that you are more than what you do, more than what happens

to you, more than your cherished commentaries! To be at peace

and a presence for peace — this is the heart of equanimity. With

equanimity, you realize that what is said and what is done — even if

directed at you — need not be taken personally and reactively.

In my lake analogy, when you are at the effect of the winds and

ripples of surface thinking, you are tugged "to and fro" by every

fear and desire. All of these external factors energize your little,

fearful, unsatisfied self. Breathe. Return to the fuller moment. Bring

mindfulness to bear.

Drop down to the mid-point of the lake. Then you can *"see"* the

anger, not *"be"* the anger. Then you can see the actions in the world

more clearly, not simply as a commentary on yourself! Then you can

act in a way that brings more peace to all. From the mid-point —

halfway down in the lake, you access the observing self — the part of

you that can look up to see your surface self, all too ready to react.

You can also look down to a depth dimension in you, in others, in

the world. Sensing that the lake is connected to the great ocean, you

touch the Source, the Ever-Present Origin. Glimpsing deep union

and communion, you trust more. You realize all is water. You become more transparent. Loving kindness moves through you. Communion with all suffering beings enlarges you. Deep joy shines through you. A profound sense of serenity enfolds you.

The word "equanimity" has interesting roots — east and west. In Sanskrit, the root of the word is to "look over," as on a mountaintop we can look over the situation and see various aspects, giving us an integral 360-degree perspective.[111] In English, the root comes from a balanced or even-minded spirit (aequus – balanced or even or equal; animus – spirit). Whether approached from east or west, equanimity suggests calm and clarity, serenity and steadiness, patience and peacefulness. I think of equanimity as being at peace (within) and being a peacemaker (without), cultivating peace in yourself and in the communities where you dwell.

The Great Paradox — a Tale of Two Realities that are One

Here is a chant that I call The Great Paradox Chant:

> Everything IS — quite all right; our worth secure and true
> AND
> Everything's NOT quite all right; we've worthy work to do.[112]

I think of the Zen master Shunryu Suzuki who remarked to his students: "All of you are perfect just as you are . . . . and all of you could use a little more work!" A useful paradox. We might speak of a place where two worlds meet — the world of distinctions and the world beyond distinctions. This mode of speaking is only provisional — to be written with one hand and erased with the other. In a mysterious sense, the supposed "two" worlds reflect a wholeness. In reality, there is no separation among Source, Circle of Life, and Self.

1. *Everything is quite all right — the world beyond distinctions*

When we speak of the world beyond distinctions, we are already speaking as a poet, a lover, and a fool.[113] Playfully and paradoxically. Gesturing toward something before the beginning — as if we could sense the ever-present origin where unity continually manifests as multiplicity, as a world. This is what the poet and mystic Rumi calls "the threshold where the two worlds touch" — a zone uniting time and the timeless, the born and unborn. Here, moment by moment, all is well and all manner of things are well.[114] We see a completeness in the now. The full presence of abundant life in each point and time. Perfect, yet we know not how.

2. *Everything's not quite all right — the world of distinctions*

In the world of distinctions, we experience time and movement, health and sickness, growth and stagnation, advance and decline. Here, we can declare that some ways of living are better than others: Kindness is better than cruelty, compassion is better than hatred, "peace with justice" is better than war and violence, and so on. Here we seek to reinforce skillful habits and transform unskillful ones. We amplify the movements toward health, toward growth, toward what is "still and still moving into another intensity, for a further union, a deeper communion."[115] We foster what reduces surplus suffering and promotes creative possibility for all.

Equanimity is learning to live at this juncture, this threshold.

- Breathing in, we recognize the Source and ever-surprising beauty of all beings. And we are that. As if at each moment the story is over and all is complete, nothing left out. Source, Self, and Circle of Life in a profound oneness.

- Breathing out, we participate in earth and cosmos unfolding. As if the story is beginning at each moment and we are called to amplify what is healthy and whole, to deepen life, and to transmute what is still unskillful — on the way to "the More and ever more."[116]

At this threshold, there is place for both the prophetic voice and the contemplative voice. The prophetic voice arises whenever and wherever our actions matter. And our actions always matter. So the voice of care and justice reminds those living in time of what they are called to be and do. The contemplative voice returns to silence and affirms that already and always we are home, that already and always we have all we need to live a worthy life. Since we are always invited to the depth, these moments out of time are always with us. Always they remind us that the supposed "two" worlds are one or, more modestly, "not one, not two."

Preventive Medicine: Three Possible Misunderstandings

There are at least three misunderstandings about equanimity:

1. Equanimity does not mean being emotionless. Emotions are in fact integral to being human.

2. Equanimity does not mean pretending that nothing is preferable to anything else. In the world of time and form, some ways of living are better than others.

3. Equanimity does not mean being changeless — as if life were fixed and relationships static.

Equanimity and Emotions

The near enemy of equanimity is indifference.[117] A cold detachment. A wall of isolation. A futile attempt to protect ourselves from hurt by refusing to connect with, to care for, to love, to enjoy what is ever fragile, ever changing. In the larger sense, it is a refusal to honor the emotions.[118]

All four aspects of wholeness have emotional tones. Without affection, how would we recognize love? Without empathy for the suffering of our fellow fragile creatures, how would we know compassion? Without gratefulness issuing in joy, how would we smile at our brothers and sisters in the human and the natural world? Without caring for peace and harmony, how would we be at peace and for peace?

The Buddha is often seen as having overcome emotions. I believe that this is also a misunderstanding.[119] The issue is not to extinguish feelings — even strong feelings. The way to equanimity is to notice and attend to the feelings in a mindful way and, where needed, to transform them or allow them to transform on their own.

Thich Nhat Hanh once heard news of a young girl raped by
sea pirates off the coast of Vietnam. The girl was so ashamed she
jumped overboard and drowned. Hearing this, the gentle monk felt
anger well up within him. He brought mindfulness to that arising.
He looked deeply so as to understand in a 360-degree way. The
result of his grappling with that incident was the poem "Please call
me by my true names." In the poem Thây writes:

> I am the 12-year-old girl, refugee
>   on a small boat,
> who throws herself into the ocean after
>   being raped by a sea pirate,
> and I am the pirate, my heart not yet capable
>   of seeing and loving.[120]

Equanimity and Ethics

One evening, an old Cherokee told his grandson about a
battle that goes on inside people. "The battle," he said, "is
between two wolves inside us all. One is Evil — it is anger,
envy, jealousy, sorrow, regret, greed, arrogance, self-pity,
guilt, resentment, inferiority, lies, false pride, superiority,
and ego. The other is Good — it is joy, peace, love, hope,

serenity, humility, kindness, benevolence, empathy, generosity, truth, compassion, and faith."

The grandson asked his grandfather, "Which wolf wins?"
The old man replied, simply, "The one you feed!"[121]

This story still speaks to us. The tendencies we feed will grow. Thich Nhat Hanh moves beyond a simple good and evil by shifting the metaphor to seeds in a garden. He notes that each of us has the seeds of all tendencies and traits within us. We have the seeds of Hitler and Stalin and the seeds of Gandhi and Mother Teresa. Some seeds are beneficial to us and to the whole. Other seeds are destructive to us and to all. Realizing this, we are called to good "seed watering." In the garden, other things being equal, the seeds that flourish are the seeds we water.

Seed watering brings us back to ethics. I consider ethics to be a set of reminders of who we are — as we journey in time, as we journey together. Are your actions and mine honoring the ancestors and serving the children? Is what we do and how we live reducing unnecessary suffering and promoting creative possibility for all? The Rotary Club has a simple yet inclusive "Four-Way Test of the Things We Think, Say, or Do":

Is it the truth?
Is it fair to all concerned?
Will it build good will and better friendship?
Will it be beneficial to all concerned?[122]

Of course, these touchstones still require wise judgment and constant evaluation, yet they point the way — simple steps arising from an expansive heart. In fact, in these chapters I have been inviting us

- to favor love and loving kindness over hate and greed
- to favor sensitivity to suffering and the impulse to alleviate it over cruelty and indifference
- to favor gratefulness and joy over ingratitude, resentment, and despair
- to favor being at peace and promoting peace over being reactive and promoting violence and discord

Any ethics worthy of us will include the possibility of self-revision. Theologian and philosopher Bernard Lonergan gives us what he calls the Transcendental Imperatives: *"Be attentive. Be insightful. Be reasonable. Be responsible. Develop and, if necessary, change."* Here is a sketch of healthy, revisable, knowing and growing.[123] When we are on the path of self-correcting learning, we develop. When we are not in alignment with this dynamism, we need to reverse the process and get back on track. In this way we extend the healthy and wholesome; we transmute the unhealthy and unwholesome.

Equanimity and Dynamic Equilibrium

> Ever changing, never less than whole.
> Ever present, never twice the same.

Artist and designer Robert Irwin placed these words on a plaque at the garden he designed for the Getty Museum outside of Los Angeles.

Coming from interconnection with the Source, we begin with mystery, with a fruitful unknowing. All is far more beautiful than we can imagine. At the threshold between time and the timeless, we embrace both change and the changeless. We welcome impermanence as part of the mystery. The "pain of choosing at every step"[124] is also the joy of responding to "beauty, ever ancient, ever new."[125]

A well-known saying counsels: "If you wish for peace, work for justice." The opposite is also true: "To seek justice, walk in peace."[126] This means developing the capacity to love our enemies and, at the limit, not to have enemies. People are not the positions they take, even though the positions — translated into policies — can cause great harm. So the examples of peace and reconciliation of Archbishop Tutu and Nelson Mandela, of Gandhi and King, lead us on. As only love overcomes hate, so only being at peace allows us to seek peace peacefully.

Concluding Words

Here are some steps toward peace within and without:

- ❧ Reduce reactivity — Stop, look, and listen before responding.
- ❧ Reduce stories about self and others — The reality of each of us is richer than the stories we tell about ourselves and others, richer than our personal and our collective stories. Reducing the power of such stories allows us to see the complexity in ourselves, in others, and in what binds us together. We are each so much more than the positions we take. Listening from the heart and to the heart is a courageous way of waging peace.
- ❧ Recommit to peace as the way — Being at peace and for peace is the fruit of practice. When there is stillness within,

we can come from interconnection and together discover
what is good for the whole and fair to each participant-
part.[127]

Often we are tempted to react in old ways that continue the stories
we know are too small to live in. Suppose instead we were to heed
the more excellent way that Rumi suggests in his poem, "The Guest
House":

> This being human is a guest house.
> Every morning a new arrival.
> A joy, a depression, a meanness,
> some momentary awareness comes
> as an unexpected visitor.
> Welcome and entertain them all!
> Even if they're a crowd of sorrows,
> who violently sweep your house
> empty of its furniture
> still, treat each guest honorably.
> He may be clearing you out
> for some new delight.
> The dark thought, the shame, the malice,

meet them at the door laughing,
and invite them in.
Be grateful for whoever comes,
because each has been sent
as a guide from beyond. [128]

Then might we not also know what the rabbi from Nazareth taught us: "Blessed are the peacemakers, for they shall be called the children of God"?[129]

Afterword

I am so small. How can this great love be in me?
Look at your eyes. They are small.
They see enormous things.[130]

— Rumi

I count it a privilege to have devoted a year to practicing the Fourfold Path and dwelling in this company. Now is the moment to harvest some lessons learned in accepting the invitation (1) *to love and extend loving kindness*, (2) *to acknowledge suffering and alleviate it*, (3) *to receive life as gift and, being grateful, to rejoice in it*, and (4) *to be at peace and to promote peace*.

Five Lessons

First, just as we can think of Source under the aspect of person and under the aspect of natural forces,[131] so I have come to view the Fourfold (love, compassion, joy, peace) in a dual fashion — somewhat like particles and waves:

As personal qualities

As dynamics associated
with nature unfolding

love, compassion, joy, peace

fire, water, air, earth

Thinking in this way keeps us mindful of the human realm and also the natural world.

Second, the Fourfold Path is itself an interweaving — each aspect balancing and enriching each. Practicing one leads to practicing all. Coming to understand the four as intertwined helps us to think more generally in terms of interconnection, interdependence, interbeing.[132] It encourages us to think of ourselves and others as holons — i.e., wholes that are also parts of larger wholes.[133] This aids us to break the spell of separateness and to see the wholeness of the garden as well as the plants within it. Even in one-to-one relationships we can "see two and think three" — the relational field and the parties within it. Cultivating all three provides triple satisfaction.[134] It reminds us of each level of community, to seek what is good for the whole and fair to the participant-parts.

Third, the Fourfold Path includes within it an ethical dimension, an ecological dimension, and an ecumenical dimension. The ethical was explicitly discussed in the chapters on compassion and peace. The ecological is associated with the elements and with expanding our notion of the Circle of Life. The ecumenical (dialogue among spiritual traditions) entered with the realization that the Fourfold resonated with wisdom traditions old and new, east and west. I called the quartet a transreligious treasure.

Fourth, if we think in terms of holons, then practicing the Fourfold simply at the interpersonal level is not enough. The Fourfold — as modes of dwelling and as aspects of earth unfolding — need to take root at a set of nested levels:

- interpersonal partnerships,
- families and the relationships within them,
- organizations — with their corporate cultures, their people, policies, and procedures,[135]
- nations with the various sub-groupings within them,
- international organizations — both of nation states, transnational corporations, and non-governmental organizations (NGOs),
- the planet itself situated in a still-unfolding universe.

The Fourfold Path is good medicine wherever practiced. In any situation, we will benefit the whole and its participants, if we

increase our love, receiving and sharing;

increase our compassion, receiving and sharing;

increase our joy, receiving and sharing;

increase our peace and equanimity, receiving and sharing.

Yet further questions await us. How, at each level, can we act more lovingly, compassionately, joyfully, and peacefully — with care for all our kin over generations? How can the Fourfold percolate through our collective thinking at each level, including the institutional policies that affect all? How can the implicit ethics, the ecological imperatives, and the cross-cultural wisdom in the Fourfold call each level to its deeper nature?

Fifth, a first intertwining deals with the explicitly ecological context — how to expand our notion of the Circle of Life.[136] A second intertwining concerns how Circle of Life and Source and Self are themselves intertwined and how enlarging each affects all. To these fruitful themes, let us now turn.

The First Intertwining — Ecology and the Circle of Life

Joanna Macy speaks of "The Great Turning" of our times.[137] Thomas Berry speaks of "The Great Work."[138] Suppose we practice the Fourfold Path in a very large consciousness—an awareness of the earth unfolding in the context of the universe story. My three mantras place the four modes of dwelling in that larger frame:

> I do not do the Great Work for myself alone.
>> My good is intertwined with the good of all my kin.
> I do not do the Great Work by myself alone.
>> Others companion me; I can ask for and receive help.
> I do not do the Great Work by my own powers alone.
>> I participate in the energies of life itself and the universe evolving.

In this wider worldview, what does the Fourfold Path ask of us?

Love or Loving Kindness

To practice love or loving kindness asks us to stop, to be calm, and to look deeply into the good of another — for the other's own sake and for the sake of the whole.[139] When I come from interconnection in the context of the earth community, I begin first to realize how deeply I and my fellow humans are intertwined. Then I realize how deeply I and all beings are intertwined. When I invoke the spirit of the Great Mystery, I realize that I do not understand another's good nor does the other fully understand his or her good. With awareness, we come to see a "creative third" — how the relationship itself is a good, how it serves the partners within it and contributes beyond itself. So we enter inquiry together — lovingly — so as to find a way. Letting go of control and creating the conditions to inquire together allows us to tend the relationship itself, those within it, and all who are gifted when the relationship is healthy and whole. Here I modify somewhat four mantras first suggested by Thich Nhat Hanh:

> Darling, I am here for you, with you.
>
> Darling, I recognize that you are here and I am very happy.
>
> Darling, I wonder if you are suffering/having difficulties. I am here. May I help?
>
> Darling, I'm suffering. I need your help.[140]

I present these to underline how love encourages reciprocity — the "to and fro" of dialogue, the surprising nature of inquiry, and a call to "think partnership first and then you and me."[141] This seen, we realize the need to bring deep listening and loving speech to our relationships and all they serve. A final test case for love is to love our enemies and at the limit not to have enemies.

Compassion

Compassion brings us face to face with suffering. Compassion calls us to a deep solidarity with all our kin. To open the heart of compassion is to learn "to care and not to care."[142] This means once more that we *stop, look, and listen* — this time in the presence of suffering and fragility. Doing so, we realize "how fragile we are." We realize we are "foolish beings of wayward passions," capable of hurting and being hurt, intentionally and unintentionally.[143] We become sensitive to individual and collective suffering. We learn from all our kin how to relieve suffering, when we can, and how to bear it together, when we must. A test case for compassion is to do good to those whom we find difficult, who may have hurt us. In such a school of compassion, we become healing presences to one another —reducing unnecessary suffering and promoting creative possibility for our common life.

Joy

When we experience life as pure gift, we lessen the tendency to control life. A grateful heart rejoices, and the joy is expansive, moving like wind in all directions. *"Bonum est diffusivum sui,"* said the medieval thinkers. *The good diffuses itself*. It moves by its nature to share and to celebrate. A test case for joy is sympathetic joy — the ability to rejoice in the good of another. Practice in doing this reminds us again that we are intertwined. Deep joy — below the surface opposites of happiness and sorrow, pleasure and pain — vibrates like the strings of a musical instrument and resonates throughout the network of all beings.

Peace or Equanimity

When we move to stillness within, we are able to open the eyes and ears of the heart. When we are at peace, we can be a presence for peace. We do this first and foremost by acting lovingly and compassionately, joyfully and peacefully. Together with others, we can discern what is to be done and not to be done. When we come from interconnection in the spirit of the Great Mystery, we move toward a harmony as yet unknown. Imagination and creativity enter. Steps of respect and listening emerge. The mud settles and possibility rises. A test case for being at peace and promoting peace is to exercise a prophetic voice without breaking the bonds of solidarity, without losing sight of what we have in common at the deepest level.

The Second Intertwining: The Circle of Life, the Source, and Our Deep Self

Our next step is to explore how the Circle of Life, Source, and Self are themselves deeply intertwined.

The Fourfold and the Circle of Life

> I meet the sun without/within,
>> sharing light and warmth with all my kin,
> I meet the sea without/within,
>> sharing water's way with all my kin.
> I meet the air without/within,
>> sharing breath and joy with all my kin.
> I meet the earth without/within,
>> sharing solid ground with all my kin.

Here I am suggesting that we become bilingual — able to express the four powers in the language of human qualities: love, compassion, joy, and peace and also in the symbolic language of the four elements: fire, water, air, and earth.

Yet we can go further. By following Brian Swimme, we can place the four elements in an evolving cosmic context. We can imagine each of the four powers having a range of expression from (a) minerals through (b) plants and (c) animals to (d) humans.

- *The seeds of love lie in attraction or allurement.* Fire from sun to hearth is a symbol for this cosmic attraction — this longing that becomes belonging.
- *The seeds of compassion lie in sensitivity.* Water with its power of absorbing and assimilating is a symbol for this cosmic sensitivity.
- *The seeds of joy lie in movement and energy.* Gentle wind and life-giving air moving outward to announce, share, and celebrate are symbols of this cosmic power which spills over into joy.
- *The seeds of peace germinate as new patterns seeking dynamic balance.* The stable creative earth that keeps making a home for all beings is a symbol of this cosmic power to be at peace and to foster peace.[144]

Think of participating in:

- the power of fire's allurement to move us to union;
- the power of water's sensitivity to bring us to empathize with each being in its setting, acknowledging its fragility, suffering, and pain;

- the power of wind's essential sharing, spreading life and joy without, and the breath of life within;
- the power of earth's equanimity — coming to stillness and presencing peace.

How do we enlarge our sense of the Circle of Life? Recall that it is as easy as one-two-three:

1. Expand the circle from *"some humans"* as valuable to *"all humans"* as valuable.
2. Expand the circle from *"humans alone"* as valuable in themselves and their relationships to *"all beings"* as valuable in themselves and their relationships.
3. Expand the circle from all beings at this time having value to all beings over all times having value — the ancestors and contemporaries and those yet-to-be of all species.

In this way, we realize how deeply we are intertwined with all beings. We know deeply that what is done to one group or species affects all. We come to love all our kin and learn from the earth how to sustain life in adaptive ways.

My Celtic ancestors might offer a blessing for the work:

May the fire of love be ours.

May the water of sensitive compassion be ours.

May the wind song of joy be ours.

May the fertile earth ground us and bring us peace.

The Fourfold and Source

When we relate through love, we see the depth dimension[145] as personal. We see our relation to the Ultimate as an "I –Thou" relation.[146] The more we approach in love, the more the subject of our love is personalized. ***This is the way of devotion.***

When we see the Great Mystery as the dynamic pattern of the universe, as the Tao, as the "inside of the inside" of all things,[147] as the forces that move through all things, then we participate in the primal forces, becoming co-workers in the world's unfolding. We seek to serve the One and to serve all beings in that oneness. ***This is the way of compassion or service.***

When we see the Great Mystery as giving all as gift, we respond in gratefulness and we rejoice. ***This is the way of thanksgiving and joy.***

When in stillness we calm ourselves, we see the depth dimension of everything more clearly. We hear the call to be stewards of earth and builders of community. We witness the communion of all beings — human and other-than-human. ***This is the way of wisdom and of peace.***

Through these several approaches, we keep enlarging our sense of the Source or Great Mystery.

The Fourfold and the Self

My small-minded self — my ripple self — is partial, asleep, enslaved, and reactive. My witness self — imaged as being at mid-level of the lake—stops, looks, and listens. This witness self is already more whole, more awake, more free, more "response-able," i.e., more able to choose a response. As I move to my deepest Self, I realize all is water. I am at one with the Source and with all other beings. I am more and more transparent to the Great Mystery manifesting in all that is.[148]

Undoing Our Stories

So far we have seen that the issues of our day are calling us to keep enlarging our sense of the Circle of Life, our sense of the Source, and our sense of our deep Self.

Why did we think we needed to do this? Because we believed a cultural story along these lines:

> Sometime, somewhere: A split developed between the Source and creation. God became more and more remote, more unlike us, wholly other. Even when we knew that the Source was closer to ourselves than we were to ourselves, still the image of a separate God persisted.[149]

> Sometime, somewhere: Splits developed within the Circle of Life — between humans and humans, between humans and the rest of creation, and between this generation and past and future generations. Humans became the measure of all values, and the other animals, the plants, and the minerals were seen as valuable only in serving the human ones.

> Sometime, somewhere: A split developed within people's awareness — under the spell of separateness, Self detached from the Circle of Life, and Self detached from Source.

Certainly we need to heal the splits in our own awareness and conduct, especially where such ways of dwelling in separateness are causing so much destruction. Such undertakings are worthy.

Yet suppose we tell the other side of the story. In reality there are not these splits and never have been. The earth goes on in its interconnected way. The troublesome splits emerged in language while the illusions went unquestioned. Our collective thinking has made it so!

Suppose we were to see the alleged boundaries as but lines on water. That would mean a different sort of return — a return to what, in a real sense, always was and still is at the deepest level.

The Source and the Universe are not two separate realities. The Source and our deep Self are not two separate realities. The Universe and every being are in the Source, and Source is in the Universe and every being.

The Circle of all Life is a communion of subjects, all profoundly interconnected in space and over generations. I am in them and they in me. The Source is in them, and they are in the Source.

My deep Self is not separate from the Circle of all beings. I am in them and they in me. Nor is my deep Self separate from the Source — I am in the Source, and the Source is in me.

Let us continue, by all means, enlarging our notion of the Circle of Life, our Source, and our deep Self. Yet know that we are also disassembling illusions. Letting go and letting be. Letting the Universe be the Universe, the Source be Source. Letting each Self remember its true nature. With less effort, more like circling round and round like a hawk riding the thermals.

We have a compass with four directions. And we can make a commitment that cannot fail, namely, a commitment to act more lovingly, more compassionately, more joyfully, and more peacefully. For how are we to respond to harsh times if not by increasing our love and loving kindness, deepening our compassion, sharing our deepest joy, and being at peace and for peace?

- ☙ In the fire of love, expressing loving kindness.
- ☙ In the spirit of water, dissolving into waters of compassion, being more sensitive to others in their fragility, their capacity to hurt and be hurt, to cause and alleviate suffering.
- ☙ In the spirit of ever-nourishing air, being more attentive to all as gift with a response of gratefulness and joy. A joy like the wind — subtle, powerful, radiating out in celebration.

❧ In the spirit of earth, being more at peace within and a stand for peace without — solid as a mountain, fertile as a meadow.

Thich Nhat Hanh sees the four as arising from our enlightened nature. And he tends to speak of the four as aspects of love.[150] As we conclude this turning of the spiral path, we might end with this poem of Rumi:

> Without love, there will be no joy and no festivity in the world.
> Without love, there will be no true living and no harmony.
> If a hundred raindrops pour down from the clouds to the sea
> Without love's doing, a pearl will not form in the deepest water.[151]

❦ 99 ❦

Perhaps, if you turn the pearl slowly and look with the eye of the heart, you will see images and hear echoes of love and compassion, joy and peace. How could it be otherwise?

Notes

1. Quoted from Rumi's poem, "The Root of the Root of Yourself," translated by Kabir Helminski. For the full poem, see Kabir Helminski, *Love is a Stranger* (Putney, VT: Threshold Books, 1993), pp. 16–17.

2. I came across the term "kindom" in reading a book by a colleague, Rebecca Todd Peters, *In Search of the Good Life: The Ethics of Globalization* (New York: Continuum, 2004). Professor Peters writes: "I embrace Ada Maria Isasi-Diaz's transformation of the concept of 'kingdom' and its patriarchal, hierarchical connotations to the concept of 'kindom,' which represents the 'kinship of all creation and the promise of a just future.' See Ada Maria Isasi-Diaz, *Mujerista Theology: A Theology for the Twenty-first Century* (Maryknoll, NY: Orbis Books, 1996), 103 n8." The comments occur in Peters' book on p. 33, endnote 16 to chapter 2. I choose to hyphenate the word as "kin-dom."

3. In a Christian context, the kingdom or reign of God that Jesus proclaims is already present at the depth and ever in process of being realized in the manifest world. For a striking exposition of this "already" and "not yet," see Jay G. Williams, *Yeshua Buddha* (Wheaton, IL: Theosophical Publishing House, 1978).

4. For a beautiful treatment of the four elements, see Christine Valters Paintner, *Water, Wind, Earth and Fire: The Christian Practice of Praying with the Elements* (Notre Dame, IN: Sorin Books, 2010). I shall later propose a way of moving back and forth between the Fourfold presented here and the four elements. I correlate (a) love with fire (ever present, ever changing); (b) compassion with water (capable of absorbing what it touches, dissolving barriers and allowing empathy to emerge); (c) joy with air (capable of entering into us through breath, capable of diffusing itself like celebration); and (d) peace with earth (capable of fertility, stability, harmony, and renewal).

5. Blake minces no words, writing: "May God us keep from Single Vision and Newton's sleep!"

6. For Blake, see Harold C. Goddard, *Blake's Fourfold Vision* — Pendle Hill Pamphlet #86 (Lebanon, PA: Sowers Printing Company — originally given as a lecture at

Swarthmore College, October 1935; copyright Pendle Hill, 1956; Library of Congress catalog number 56-7354).

7. On Heidegger, see Martin Heidegger's essay "Building Dwelling Thinking," in his *Poetry, Language, Thought*, trans. Alfred Hofstadter (New York: Harper and Row, 1971; Colophon paperback edition, 1975), pp. 145–161.

8. On the Four Dwellings, also called the Four Immeasurable Minds, see Thich Nhat Hanh, *Teachings on Love* (Berkeley, CA: Parallax Press, 1998), pp. 1–9, and also *The Heart of the Buddha's Teaching* (New York: Broadway Books, 1999), pp. 169–175. For another rich treatment, see Sharon Salzberg, *Loving-Kindness: The Revolutionary Art of Happiness* (Boston: Shambhala Press, 1995).

9. I borrow this lovely phrase from the work of Brother David Steindl-Rast.

10. Matt. 7:20.

11. Gal. 5:22.

12. In the other Religions of the Book, a motif is mercy. Justice and mercy in Judaism: "What does the Lord require of you but that you do justice, love mercy and walk humbly with your God?" (Micah 6:8). And each chapter (save one) of the holy Qur'an begins with the phrase: "In the name of Allah, The Compassionate, the Merciful."

13. The near enemies appear in the text below. For an overlapping treatment of the near enemies, see Jack Kornfield, *A Path with a Heart* (New York: Bantam Books, 1993), pp.190–191.

14. Here I am following David Brazier. See his *Zen Therapy* (New York: John Wiley & Sons, 1995), pp. 93–94, and also chapters 17 and 18. I realize that there is also a case for considering hate as the opposite of love. As the Buddha said: "Only love can overcome hate. This is an eternal law." See the *Dhammapada*.

15. When we choose to believe that we live in scarcity rather than sufficiency, when we falsely believe that power, possessions, and prestige define us, then others appear as threats to diminish our worth. We live in a world of pernicious comparison. Even when we reject superiority and inferiority, we mistake equality for a kind of "keeping score." Such comparison does not allow us to take joy in the good of others.

16. For a fuller treatment of this move from modernity with its spell of separateness to an ecological worldview emphasizing interconnection, see my *Living Large: Transformative Work at the Intersection of Ethics and Spirituality* (Laurel, MD: Tai Sophia Press, 2004).

17. The circle is multilayered in that it does not simply encompass individuals. The four powers are forces for wholeness and find expression at all levels — interpersonal, familial, institutional, regional, national, international, and planetary.

18. The phrase comes from the West Wall Inscription from the office of Chang Tsai, an eleventh-century administrator in China, which reads: "Heaven is my father and earth is my mother and even such a small creature as I find an intimate place in its midst. That which extends throughout the universe I regard as my body. That which directs the universe I regard as my nature. All people are my brothers and sisters. And all things are my companions." See William Theodore de Bary, Wing-Tsit Chan and Burton Watson, *Sources of Chinese Tradition*, Vol. I (New York: Columbia University Press, 1960), p. 469.

19. The quote: "Homo sum, humani nihil a me alienum puto" is from Terence's play, *Heauton Timorumenos* (The Self-Tormentor).

20. See his "Canticle of the Sun."

21. I take the name "the Great Family" from Gary Snyder's poem, "Prayer for the Great Family," which he tells us is "after a Mohawk Prayer." In the poem, Snyder expresses gratitude to Mother Earth, to Plants, to Air, to Wild Beings, to Water, to the Sun, and to the Great Sky. See Gary Snyder, *Turtle Island* (New York: New Directions Books, 1969, 1974), pp. 24–25.

22. In many places, Thomas Berry urges us to relate to the natural world — "not as a collection of objects but as a communion of subjects." See, for example, his *The Great Work* (New York: Bell Tower, 1999), pp. 16 and 82.

23. This image was a favorite of my mentor, Frederick Franck. See, for example, Frederick Franck, *A Little Compendium on That Which Matters* (New York: St. Martin's Press, 1993) and his *The Icon Reborn*, with photography by Luz Piedad Lopez (New York: Pacem in Terris, 2005).

24. Think also of the Cosmic Christ, the Kabbalah's Great Tree of Life, the Mahayana Buddhist teaching on the three bodies of the Buddha.

25. The poem is called "Outwitted." See Edwin Markham, *The Shoes of Happiness and Other Poems* (Garden City, NY: Doubleday, Page and Company, 1915).

26. I first noticed this idea of going beyond fight or flight in Richard Rohr's book, *Hope Against Darkness: The Transforming Vision of Saint Francis in an Age of Anxiety* (Cincinnati, OH: St. Anthony Messenger Press, 2001). The particular formulation used here is my own.

27. The first full lines of American poet e. e. cummings' poem "Be of love (a little) more careful than of everything." See e. e. cummings, *Complete Poems: 1904–1962*, ed. George J. Firmage (New York: Liveright, 1991), p. 453. This poem originally appeared in e. e. cummings, *No Thanks*, p. 68.

28. Often the phrase loving kindness is written as one word: "lovingkindness." This does echo the Hebrew "hesed." However, I prefer to accent both the "loving" aspect and the "kindness" aspect and so choose to keep the words distinct.

29. The original says: "When I do not know who you are, I serve you. When I know who you are, I am you." However, I think this is already at a more advanced level. To me, the starting point is more likely to be when I am in deeper ignorance and highly ego-centric. Then I manipulate you, i.e., I am willing to persuade you to do what I want, against your will and best interest, using techniques of deception and/or coercion. For more on these matters, see my *Living Large: Transformative Work at the Intersection of Ethics and Spirituality*, Appendix VII, pp. 253–256.

30. As is increasingly familiar, the modes of manipulation are many. Some manipulate by force or threat of force, others by a kind of emotional blackmail. Psychologist Frederick "Fritz" Perls distinguished Top Dog manipulators — typically using an aggressive bullying style — and Underdog manipulators — typically playing "poor me" and winning sympathy. See Fritz Perls, *Gestalt Therapy Verbatim* (New York: Bantam, 1959/1971). Perls' student Everett L. Shostrum gives four types of Top Dog and four types of Underdog manipulators. See his *Man the Manipulator* (New York: Bantam, 1968).

31. Growing up can be seen as reversing the Ego Chant in this fashion: (1) I go from me alone as measuring stick (Me!) to myself as one among others, others who have their own lives and needs and feelings and points of view. (2) I go from making my wants into needs (Me want it!) to distinguishing wants from needs. (3) I go from demanding instant gratification (Me want it now!) to learning to delay such gratification when appropriate. (4) I go from making others solely the means to my ends (Me want it regardless!) to realizing that others have rights and responsibilities, that others are owed respect, and that I cannot override such boundaries without becoming unjust to them.

32. See James Edwin Loder's book, *Human Development in Theological Perspective* (San Francisco: Jossey-Bass, 1998).

33. See M. Scott Peck, *The Road Less Traveled* (New York: Simon & Schuster, 1978).

34. The cultural critic and writer, bell hooks, in her wonderful book *All About Love* (New York: William Morrow and Company, 2000) affirms the choice to start with love as an action. She also broadens the context to see genuine love as a combination of "care, commitment, trust, knowledge, responsibility and respect." See p. 7 and again p. 94.

35. The quote is attributed to the French anthropologist and mystic, Pierre Teilhard de Chardin.

36. I hear this phrase in the voice of the Reverend Jesse Jackson, chanting: "But there is . . . a more excellent way."

37. I look at the three developmentally. While I treat eros as a feature of our embodiment and hence always present in shifting forms, there is also a sense that eros — as an urge to union — can be pre-personal, even pre-ethical. Philia as the love of friendship is personal and includes the ethical. Agape can be viewed as transpersonal and trans-ethical. Sharon Salzberg in her book *Lovingkindness* (p. 24) points out that the Pali word "metta" has two roots: One is the word "gentle" as in a gentle rain; the other is the word "friend." Furthermore, love as metta contains something of the unconditional that also marks agape.

38. See Brain Swimme, *The Universe is a Green Dragon: A Cosmic Creation Story* (Santa Fe, NM: Bear & Company, 1984).

39. On this topic, Aristotle has much to say in the West; Confucius has much to say in the East.

40. David Brazier, *Zen Therapy*, p. 201. The reach of love to unconditional love will be looked at in the section on agape. For now it is enough to note that in friendship we often are speaking of a love that has not grown all the way to unconditional. Brazier recognizes the point in distinguishing ordinary love and great love. He says: "Ordinary love is the love we have for the things and people which are important to ourselves. Great love is non-possessive and unconditional" (ibid).

41. This is my rendering. For a more literal translation, see Margaret Smith, *Rabi'a: The Life and Work of Rabi'a and Other Women Mystics in Islam* (Oxford: One World, 1994), p. 50.

42. Humility, as I see it, is to know our true size, between everything and nothing. Not superior, not inferior, not even equal in the "keeping score" sense. We participate at our core in the Great Mystery whose image and likeness shines through us when we are most transparent to the Source.

43. The phrase is that of Charles Williams who in naming "the City" names London as it is to us but also as it is to God, whose mercy adds a depth dimension, where spirit manifests the beauty in all things.

44. Also called "metta" meditation.

45. As love increases and greed lessens, we shall also see that fear dissipates. As scripture teaches, when love reaches its fullness, there is no place for fear. See 1 John 4:18: "There is no fear in love, but perfect love drives out fear."

46. See bell hooks, *All About Love*, e.g., pp. 19, 33, 72.

47. From the Christian tradition, see Matt. 7:20.

48. See Gal. 5:22: "What the Spirit produces is love, joy, peace, patience, kindness, goodness, faithfulness, gentleness, self-control."

49. This is my own version of St. Paul, drawing on a number of translations and at times drawing out a meaning by adding an equivalent phrase. I offer it respectfully — not to replace but to illuminate the much-loved passage. To compare with the original in a number of translations, go to http://bible.cc/1 Corinthians 13.

50. These words come from a prayer that St. Richard of Chichester prayed on his death-bed: "*Thanks be to Thee, my Lord Jesus Christ. For all the benefits Thou hast given me. For all the pains and insults Thou hast borne for me. O most merciful Redeemer, friend and brother. May I know Thee more clearly, Love Thee more dearly, Follow Thee more nearly.*" The play "Godspell" incorporates the quote in its song "Day by Day," asking "to see Thee more clearly, to love Thee more dearly, to follow Thee more nearly — day by day."

51. From the song "Fragile" — words and music by Sting. See A&M label, CD *Nothing Like the Sun* © 1987. In the liner notes, Sting pays tribute to the 27-year-old American engineer Ben Linder who was killed by the U.S.-supported Contras in Nicaragua. Fourteen years later, on September 11, 2001, the day of the attack on the World Trade Center and Pentagon, Sting was preparing to do an evening Webcast concert from Tuscany, Italy. Instead of cancelling the concert, he told his fans: "We are performing the song 'Fragile' as a prayer and a mark of respect for the people who have died or are suffering as a result of this morning's tragedy. We are shutting down the Webcast after this song."

52. See W. B. Yeats, *The Collected Poems of W. B. Yeats* (New York: Macmillan, 1956), last lines of "Among School Children," p. 214.

53. See T. S. Eliot, *The Complete Poems and Plays: 1909–1950*, The Four Quartets, "Burnt Norton," p.119.

54. My wife is Gregg Winn Sullivan. Her first name is her mother's maiden name. She and I presented a workshop, "Be Still and Know: Walking with Mystery," as part of First Parish Project VI at Hinton Rural Life Center, Hayesville, NC, November 10 and 12, 2009. The two-day workshop on spirituality was designed for 16 young ministers from all over the U.S. This was the first time I heard her use the term "wounded miracles."

55. The story of Gotama Siddhartha is covered in many works introducing the life and teaching of the Buddha. See, for example, Samuel Bercholz and Sherab Chödzin Kohn (editors), *Entering the Stream: An Introduction to The Buddha and His Teachings* (Boston: Shambhala, 1993).

56. The English word "compassion" is made up of the verb whose root (passio/pati) means "to suffer" and the prefix (com) meaning "with." From the Buddhist tradition, the term we translate as compassion is "karuna." Thich Nhat Hanh also uses the English term "compassion"; however he is not entirely comfortable with it. He notes that a doctor can be compassionate without actually suffering the disease she is treating. See Thich Nhat Hanh, *The Heart of the Buddha's Teaching* (New York: Broadway Books, 1998), pp. 169–175.

57. For more on this distinction between necessary and unnecessary suffering, see my *Living Large: Transformative Work at the Intersection of Ethics and Spirituality*. For an alternate approach which looks at the six realms of suffering, see Martin Lowenthal and Lar Short, *Opening the Heart of Compassion* (Boston: Charles E. Tuttle Company, 1993).

58. The path is called the Eightfold Path: A. It begins with an insight/commitment phase — (i) right insight and (ii) right resolve. B. It continues with an ethical component — (iii) right speaking, (iv) right acting, and (v) right vocation. C. It completes each turn of the cycle with a meditative component — (vi) steady, (vii) mindful, (viii) concentration. All of this produces more insight and more compassionate resolve, and round and round we go — walking the spiral path of the ethical component and the meditative component for still fuller insight (becoming great wisdom) and commitment (becoming great compassion).

59. See David Brazier, *Zen Therapy*, p. 93.

60. I have written elsewhere about the need to undergird spiritual practice with ethical practice. See my *Living Large: Transformative Work at the Intersection of Ethics and Spirituality*, chapters 1–4, pp. 27–83.

61. A traditional formulation might be: (1) Don't kill. (2) Don't steal. (3) Don't engage in sexual misconduct. (4) Don't use false speech. (5) Don't use (or perhaps abuse)

intoxicants. I am modifying a version used by Thich Nhat Hanh. Some years ago, he stopped calling them "precepts" and began referring to them as "mindfulness trainings." For the fuller version I am modifying, see his *Teachings on Love* (Berkeley, CA: Parallax Press, 1998), chapter 11, especially, pp. 123–125. For an even more recent version of the Five Mindfulness Trainings with accent on interbeing and our global situation, see http://www.plumvillage.org/mindfulness-trainings/3-the-five-mindfulness-trainings.html.

62. I am thinking here of the older tradition of virtues and vices. Virtues are constructive habits of mind and heart, of attitude and behavior. Vices are destructive habits of mind and heart, of attitude and behavior.

63. The five focuses of the mindfulness trainings — (i) life, (ii) resources, (iii) sexuality, (iv) speech, and (v) consumption — are all enduring human concerns. And we can relate to each in smaller or larger mind. A small-minded way of responding increases unnecessary suffering and decreases creative possibility for our common life. A larger-minded way of responding does the opposite; it reduces surplus suffering and promotes creative possibility for our common life. For more on the notions of smaller and larger ways of relating, see my *Living Large: Transformative Work at the Intersection of Ethics and Spirituality*.

64. David Brazier makes the point that in the Zen tradition, ethics are seen as mirroring our deep nature, rather than seen as restraints needed because at base we are unruly and selfish. See David Brazier, *Zen Therapy*, pp. 36–39. Developmental level is also in play. See "Three Houses of Ethics" in my *Living Large: Transformative Work at the Intersection of Ethics and Spirituality*, pp. 68–70.

65. See Thich Nhat Hanh, *For a Future to be Possible: Commentaries on the Five Wonderful Precepts* (Berkeley, CA: Parallax Press, 1993) for further discussion of the application of the precepts on all the levels of life.

66. The most succinct version of Western ethics I know is the Rotary Club's "The Four-Way Test of the Things We Think, Say, or Do." The "test" consists of the following four questions: (1) Is it the truth? (2) Is it fair to all concerned? (3) Will it build good will and better friendship? (4) Will it be beneficial to all concerned?

67. Buddhism teaches — as a kind of summary — Five Remembrances:

 1. There is sickness and no way to escape this.
 2. There is aging and no way to escape this.
 3. There is death and no way to escape this.
 4. All we know and love will change, and there is no way to escape this.
 5. All we do will persist, and there is no way to escape this.

The wording here is mine, based on Thich Nhat Hanh's rendering in his more advanced treatise, *Understanding Our Mind* (Berkeley, CA: Parallax Press, 2006). See p. 218 ff.

68. A famous Zen story has a towering Samurai command a monk to teach him about heaven and hell. The monk insults the warrior. The warrior draws his sword to kill the insolent monk. A split second before the Samurai strikes, the monk, Hakuin, says: "That is Hell!" Amazed that the monk has gone to the brink of death to teach him, the Samurai opens his heart, experiences deep gratitude, and sheathes his sword. At this point, Hakuin says: "That is Heaven!" The teaching is that, if we are awake and alert, we have a choice in each moment of creating a bit more heaven or a bit more hell.

69. Recall that Buddhism speaks of the three poisons: (a) greed, (b) hatred, and (c) ignorance, or (a) attachment, (b) aversion, and (c) confusion, or, yet again, (a) clinging, (b) condemning, and (c) identifying with less than all we truly are. Recall also that, in Brazier's view, love and compassion are remedies to the first two poisons.

70. See David J. Brazier (aka Dharmavidya), *Who Loves Dies Well: On the Brink of Buddha's Pure Land* (Winchester, UK: O Books Division of John Hunt Publishing Ltd., 2007), p. 12.

71. I take the phrase from Jean Gebser. See his book *The Ever-Present Origin*, trans. by Noel Barstad with Algis Mickunas (Athens, OH: Ohio University Press, 1985).

72. The phrase "the Great Family" is from Gary Snyder, and by this he means all the realms: human, animal, vegetable, and mineral. See his poem "Prayer for the Great Family" in Gary Snyder, *Turtle Island* (New York: New Directions, 1974), p. 24.

73. See Thich Nhat Hanh, *Peace Is Every Step* (New York: Bantam Books, 1991), p. 95, where he writes: "If you are a poet, you will see clearly that there is a cloud floating in this sheet of paper. Without a cloud, there will be no rain; without rain, the trees cannot grow; without trees, we cannot make paper. . . . So we can say that the cloud and the paper *inter-are*. 'Interbeing' is a word that is not in the dictionary yet, but if we combine the prefix 'inter-' with the verb 'to be,' we have a new verb, 'inter-be.'"

74. Edwin Markham, "Outwitted," cited above in footnote 25.

75. I am recalling the West Wall Inscription from the office of Chang Tsai, cited above in footnote 18.

76. For a version of the full poem, translated by Jane Hirshfield, see Stephen Mitchell, editor, *The Enlightened Heart* (New York: Harper & Row, 1989), p. 102.

77. I echo the title of C. S. Lewis' book *Surprised by Joy: The Shape of My Early Life* (New York: Harcourt, Brace, 1955, 1995). For Lewis, joy points to a longing that will not be satisfied in this life.

78. My wife's name is Gregg Winn Sullivan. For 13 years, she and I co-led a course at Elon University for select juniors and seniors called "Quest for Wholeness." She also served from 1985–2000 as Associate Director of the Wesley Foundation at the University of North Carolina in Chapel Hill, where her work included counseling, social issue programming, and organizing work teams.

79. Of course, a similar point can be made by distinguishing types of happiness, for example, happiness for reasons and happiness for no reason. For a treatment that takes the latter route, see Marci Shimoff with Carol Kline, *Happy for No Reason: 7 Steps to Being Happy from the Inside Out* (New York: Free Press, 2008). Joy and "happiness for no reason" are not quite the same, yet they share a number of characteristics.

80. The song "Sometimes I'm Happy (Sometimes I'm Blue)" is from the Broadway musical "Hit the Deck" (1927) with music by Vincent Youmans and lyrics by Irving Caesar.

81. This is true of all four. Beyond liking and disliking lies a greater love. Beyond pleasure and pain lies a greater compassion. Beyond benefit and loss lies a greater joy. Beyond the impermanence of life lies a greater peace.

82. In these reflections, as will be seen later, I am indebted to Byron Katie on letting go; to the Benedictine monk Brother David Steindl-Rast for his work on gratefulness; and to Thich Nhat Hanh for his reminders on smiling and enjoying our practices. See, for example, Byron Katie with Stephen Mitchell, *Loving What Is: Four Questions that Can Change your Life* (New York: Harmony Books, 2002) and *A Thousand Names for Joy* (New York: Harmony Books, 2007). See, for example, David Steindl-Rast, *Gratefulness, The Heart of Prayer: An Approach to Life in Fullness* (New York: Paulist Press, 1984). See, for example, Thich Nhat Hanh, *Teaching on Love* (Berkeley, CA: Parallax Press, 1998).

83. Mirza Ghalib (1797–1869) was a classical Urdu and Persian poet from India.

84. Psalm 42:7. "Deep calls to deep in the roar of your waterfalls; all your waves and breakers sweep over me."

85. See Dag Hammarskjöld, "A Room of Quiet" (New York: United Nations, 1971), opening sentence. The meditation room was re-opened in 1957 at the United Nations Headquarters in New York City. Hammarskjöld had given a great deal of thought as to how the space would be shaped.

86. As Dante in Paradise navigates by the increasing beauty of Beatrice's smile, so can we experience our lives in the context of joy increasing.

87. Quoted in Marci Shimoff with Carol Kline, *Happy for No Reason*, p. 1.

88. The translation is by John Stevens. See his *Dewdrops on a Lotus Leaf: Zen Poems of Ryōkan* (Boston: Shambhala Press, 1993), also his *One Robe, One Bowl: The Zen Poetry of Ryōkan* (New York: Weatherhill, 1977, 1980) and his *Three Zen Masters: Ikkyū, Hakuin, Ryōkan* (Tokyo: Kodansha International, 1993). For a beautiful dialogue with the Japanese poet, see the work of the Benedictine nun, Mary Lou Kownacki, *Between Two Souls: Conversations with Ryōkan* (Grand Rapids, Michigan: Wm. B. Eerdmans

Publishing Company, 2004). Her engagement with the above poem can be found on pp. 134–135.

89. For more on the phrase "wounded miracles," see my chapter on compassion.

90. This lovely name for God or the Whole — "the More and ever more" — I take from David Steindl-Rast. I came across this way to characterize the divine in a lecture clip "Three Ways We Find the Divine" by Brother David Steindl-Rast, 2007. See http://www.youtube.com/watch?v=DZ6O-tVywnI

91. On "Wandering Joy" in Meister Eckhart, see Reiner Schurmann, *Wandering Joy: Meister Eckhart's Mystical Philosophy* (Great Barrington, MA: Lindisfarne Books, 2001). See also John S. Dunne, *The Homing Spirit: A Pilgrimage of the Mind, of the Heart, of the Soul* (New York: Crossroads, 1987), p. 71 and Meister Eckhart on the "wayless way" quoted in Bruce Chatwin, *The Songlines* (New York: Elisabeth Sifton Books, Viking, 1987), p. 179, where Chatwin also quotes the Buddha's last words: "Walk on."

92. An old Bedouin met Lawrence of Arabia in the desert and said to him: "The Love is from God and of God and towards God." See T. E. Lawrence, *Seven Pillars of Wisdom* (Harmondsworth, UK: Penguin & Jonathan Cape, 1971), p. 1. We can say something similar about the compassion, the joy, and the peace.

93. 1 Thessalonians 5:16. Paul writing in prison says: "Rejoice in the Lord always; again I will say, rejoice!" (Phil. 4:4).

94. See Thich Nhat Hanh, *Being Peace* (Berkeley, CA: Parallax Press, 1987), p. 5.

95. My guide here is the Benedictine monk, Brother David Steindl-Rast. See especially his books *Gratefulness, The Heart of Prayer: An Approach to Life in Fullness* (New York: Paulist Press, 1984) and *A Listening Heart: The Spirituality of Sacred Sensuousness*, newly revised (New York: Crossroads, 1983; revised version, 1999). Also see Robert Aitken and David Steindl-Rast, ed. Nelson Foster, *The Ground We Share: Everyday Practice, Buddhist and Christian* (Liguori, MO: Triumph Books,1994); Fritjof Capra and David Steindl-Rast with Thomas Matus, *Belonging to the Universe: Explorations on the Frontiers of Science and Spirituality* (San Francisco: HarperSanFrancisco, 1991), and David

Steindl-Rast with Sharon Lebell, *Music of Silence: A Sacred Journey through the Hours of the Day* (Berkeley, CA: Seastone, 1998).

96. Quoted on his Web site http://www.gratefulness.org.

97. As mentioned, I came across this lovely way to characterize the divine in a lecture clip "Three Ways We Find the Divine" by Brother David Steindl-Rast, 2007. See http://www.youtube.com/watch?v=DZ6O-tVywnI

98. The wisdom tradition of India speaks of satchitananda. "Sat" — a word for being, "Chit" — a word for consciousness or awareness, "Ananda" — a word for bliss. Hence, we might say that, at the heart of being, is awareness and also bliss. This is much like the medieval philosophers of the west who spoke of transcendental terms such as the one = the real = the true = the good = the beautiful. Surely the mystery here echoes the mystery of sat-chit-ananda.

99. We speak, for example, of Nature as revelatory, of the Tao, of the Spirit within, of the Buddha nature, of the Christ nature, of "that of God" in everyone.

100. See William Blake, "Auguries of Innocence," in *Selected Poetry and Prose of Blake*, ed. Northrop Frye (New York: Modern Library, 1953), p. 90.

101. Even in family relationships, mothers may become jealous of daughters, fathers jealous of sons, siblings jealous of one another.

102. I first encountered this formulation as a prelude to a ceremony inducting new members of Thich Nhat Hanh's Order of Interbeing. It is a kind of koan — leaving no place to go. To transcend the superiority complex, well yes. To transcend the inferiority complex, again, good. Then we come to the third: to transcend the equality complex. Here the trap is more subtle — comparison and scorekeeping even about what is good and holy!

103. The so-called seven deadly sins appear in Dante's "Purgatorio" as seven roots of sin or subtle obstacles to growth in love. They also appear in the advice of the great Spanish mystic, St. John of the Cross. See St. John of the Cross, *Dark Night of the Soul*, new translation and introduction by Marabai Starr (New York: Riverhead Books Division of Penguin Putnam, 2002).

104. Think of complaining, blaming, guilt-making, shaming stories. Think of the negative oppositional emotions of greed, anger, fear, envy, jealousy.

105. For more on this lake analogy, see my previous work, *Living Large: Transformative Work at the Intersection of Ethics and Spirituality*, pp. 58–62, as well as my *Spiral of the Seasons: Welcoming the Gifts of Later Life* (Chapel Hill, NC: Second Journey Publications, 2009), pp. 81–86.

106. A powerful way of releasing is what Byron Katie calls "The Work" — four questions and a "turn around":

    1. Is it true?
    2. Can you absolutely know that it's true?
    3. How do you react when you think that thought?
    4. Who would you be without that thought?

    And turn it around. For example, if one of my complaint sentences was: "My father never spent enough time with me," then I might consider its negation: "My father did have enough time for me." Or other types of "turn around": "I never had enough time for my father." Or perhaps "I never had enough time for me." Are they as true or truer than the original for me?

    For more on The Work, see Byron Katie with Stephen Mitchell, *Loving What Is: Four Questions That Can Change Your Life* (New York: Random House Harmony Books, 2002), and their volume *A Thousand Names for Joy: Living in Harmony with the Way Things Are* (New York: Random House Harmony Books, 2007), as well as *Who Would You Be Without Your Story? Dialogues with Byron Katie*, edited by Carol Williams (New York: Hay House, 2008). The Work is not without its critics, as a search of the Internet will show. Still, used in a healthy context, it is powerful.

107. This is my version of an exercise I first encountered in the work of Italian psychologist, Roberto Assagioli. See his *Psychosynthesis: A Manual of Principles and Techniques* (New York: Hobbes, Dorman, 1965).

108. See Lalla, *Naked Song*, translated by Coleman Barks (Athens, GA: Maypop Books, 1992), p. 29.

109. Eckhart Tolle, *The Power of Now* (Novato, CA: New World Library, 1999), p. 187.

110. I take this characterization from Stephen R. Covey's work. See his *The Seven Habits of Highly Effective People* (New York: Simon & Schuster Fireside Book, 1989), Habit 1. An example of reactivity is someone cutting you off in traffic, anger arising, and you finding your hand offering a rude gesture — all by itself!

111. Equanimity is *upekka* in Pali; *upeksha* in Sanskrit. The prefix "upa" means "over." And the root "iksh" means "to look," as in climbing a mountain you can look over the whole terrain. And there is a mark of upeksha called "the wisdom of equality" wherein one can understand both sides, even when one is a party to a conflict. See Thich Nhat Hanh, *The Heart of the Buddha's Teaching*, pp. 169, 174–175.

112. The accent is meant to be on the capitalized words.

113. I echo Shakespeare here: "The lunatic, the lover and the poet, are of imagination all compact." See *A Midsummer Night's Dream*, Act Five, Scene I.

114. Julian of Norwich's phrase, quoted at the end of T. S. Eliot's Four Quartets.

115. T. S. Eliot, The Four Quartets, East Coker.

116. I take this lovely phrase from the Benedictine monk, David Steindl-Rast.

117. To recap: The near enemy of love is possessiveness; the near enemy of compassion is pity; the near enemy of unselfish joy is comparison; and, as we are now exploring, the near enemy of equanimity is indifference.

118. Dan Goleman has written well of what he calls emotional intelligence. It includes character traits such as the ability to know and manage one's own feelings, to motivate self (and others), to persist, to empathize, and to read and deal effectively with other people's feelings. See Daniel Goleman, *Emotional Intelligence* (New York: Bantam Books, 1995, 1997), pp. xii, 36, and throughout.

119. In support of this view, see David Brazier, *The Feeling Buddha* (New York: Fromm International, 1997; 2000).

120. See Thich Nhat Hanh, *Call Me By My True Names: The Collected Poems of Thich Nhat Hanh* (Berkeley, CA: Parallax Press, 1999), pp. 72–73.

121. I take this telling of the tale from my colleague, David Noer. in an op-ed piece called "Which Wolf Will We Feed?" See the *Greensboro News and Record*, December 31, 2006, p. H1.

122. I want to reiterate a point made earlier: that ethical norms are meant not only for personal and interpersonal behavior, but also need to be applied communally: to relationships, to institutions (e.g. the Big Four: economic and governmental institutions, educational — including media — and religious institutions), and indeed to the planet itself in the context of the universe unfolding. Variants of the Four-Way Test can and should be applied at all these levels.

123. For this articulation of the transcendental imperatives, see David Tracy, *The Achievement of Bernard Lonergan* (New York: Herder and Herder, 1970), p. 228. For a fuller treatment, see Bernard J. F. Lonergan, *Method in Theology* (New York: Herder and Herder, 1972), p. 53 and throughout. Assessments grounded in these imperatives are to be developed. Positions at odds with this self-corrective process are to be reversed. Inattention is to be corrected by further attentiveness. Oversights corrected by further insights. Misunderstandings by further understandings. What is untested is corrected by further testing. What is irresponsible is corrected by wider and deeper responses, realizing the relevance of aspects which were earlier disregarded or misunderstood. Both what we know and what we do and even the standards by which we judge can themselves undergo review and revision.

124. U.S. Supreme Court Justice Benjamin Cardozo was fond of quoting: "We must spread the gospel that there is no gospel that will save us the pain of choosing at every step." See Benjamin Nathan Cardozo, *The Growth of the Law* (New Haven: Yale University Press, 1924), pp. 65 and 67, and again in *Selected Writings of Benjamin Nathan Cardozo*, ed. Margaret E. Hall (New York: Fallon Law Book Company, 1947), p. 380.

125. Here the echo is from St. Augustine in his *Confessions*.

126. I owe this insight to the work of Paul F. Knitter. See his book, *Without Buddha I Could Not Be a Christian* (Oxford: Oneworld Publications, 2009), Chapter 7: "Making Peace and Being Peace," pp. 167–212.

127. To explore the courage needed for waging peace in non-violent and non-demonizing ways, see West Point graduate and U.S. Army Captain Paul K. Chappell's book, *The End of War: How Waging Peace Can Save Humanity Our Planet and Our Future* (Westport, CT: Easton Studio Press, 2010).

128. See *The Essential Rumi*, translated by Coleman Barks with John Moyne, A. J. Arberry, and Reynold Nicholson (San Francisco: HarperSanFrancisco, 1995), p. 109.

129. Matt. 5:9 — part of what we have come to know as the Sermon on the Mount.

130. See Coleman Barks, translations and commentaries, *Rumi: The Book of Love* (San Francisco: HarperSanFrancisco, 2003), p. 174.

131. In the West, we tend to image the Mysterious Source along the lines of a person. Hence attributes seen in humans such as Love and Compassion, Joy and Peace, can be thought of (however inadequately) as names of God. Here we relate to the Source in an "I-Thou" manner. In the East, where nature provides a key, the Mysterious Source is imaged along the line of a force that moves through all things, giving them life and spirit, a pattern that connects, named e.g., the Mysterious Tao. Here we participate in the deep nature of the universe and all within it.

132. I have written elsewhere of the shift from the spell of separateness to a context of interbeing. See my *Living Large: Transformative Work at the Intersection of Ethics and Spirituality*, pp. 225–237. In general the move is (a) from separate selves to relational fields (interbeing — wholes that are also parts), (b) from the "seen only" to the interweaving of "seen and subtle", (c) from the short term to intergenerational time, and (d) from "superiority over" to "collaboration with" (interdoing or intercollaboration).

133. The term "holon" comes from Arthur Koestler. See his book, *The Ghost in the Machine* (New York: Macmillan, 1967), p. 48.

134. On the move beyond win-win to triple satisfaction, see my *Living Large: Transformative Work at the Intersection of Ethics and Spirituality*, pp. 253–256.

135. Think of economic, governmental, educational (including media), and religious institutions. Perhaps better, think of "for profit" and "not-for-profit" enterprises, gov-

ernmental and non-governmental agencies, formal and informal educational venues, formal religious institutions and less-explicitly-religious paths of deepening.

136. In the Opening Words of this book, I mentioned the frame of the Earth Charter which looked to three relationships: Humans to Humans; Humans to the Natural World; this Generation to Future Generations. I also spoke of expanding the circle of our care to all beings over time.

137. See Joanna Macy and Molly Young Brown, *Coming Back to Life: Practices to Reconnect Our Lives, Our World* (Gabriola Island, BC: New Society Publishers, 1998).

138. See Thomas Berry, *The Great Work: Our Way into the Future* (New York: Bell Tower, 1999).

139. I take the notion of "stopping calming and looking deeply" from Thich Nhat Hanh.

140. See Thich Nhat Hanh, *Teaching on Love*, pp. 68-72.

141. For more on this, see my *Living Large: Transformative Work at the Intersection of Ethics and Spirituality*, pp. 127-139.

142. The phrase "Teach us to care and not to care" is from the poem "Ash Wednesday," stanza I. See T. S. Eliot, *The Complete Poems and Plays: 1909–1950*, pp. 60–61.

143. The Japanese term "bombu" indicating "a foolish being of wayward passions" comes from the tradition of Pure Land Buddhism. See David Brazier (Dharmavidya), *Who Loves Dies Well: On the Brink of Buddha's Pure Land* (Winchester, UK: O Books, 2007), p. 12.

144. In this matter of showing fundamental powers over levels of manifestation, I am indebted to the work of Brian Swimme. See his book, *The Universe Is a Green Dragon: A Cosmic Creation Story*. Swimme speaks of six forces. I have adapted his insights to my purposes, making, in some cases, different correlations.

145. See previous discussion of the depth dimension on pages 50, 60, and 68.

146. See Martin Buber, *I and Thou*, trans. by Walter Kaufmann (New York: Charles Scribner's Sons, 1970).

147. The phrase is from Alan Watts.

148. For more on this lake analogy, see my book, *Living Large: Transformative Work at the Intersection of Ethics and Spirituality*, pp. 58–62.

149. In the theological language of transcendence and immanence, transcendence became dominant and was often placed in a future life, not this life. Earth, body, women, native peoples were seen as less. Disembodied spirituality, purity, non-materiality, male independence were prized. As we moved into modern times, such separations were further anchored in by what I call the Spell of Separateness. This worldview over the last 500 years emphasized (a) separate substances (separate selves) as most real. It also emphasized (b) scarcity (rather than inter-sufficiency), (c) the seen only (rather than the interweaving of seen and the subtle), (d) the short term (rather than inter-generational time), and (e) superiority over (rather than collaboration with). See my *Living Large: Transformative Work at the Intersection of Ethics and Spirituality*, pp. 273–278.

150. See Thich Nhat Hanh, *Teachings on Love*, pp. 1–9.

151. Rumi, trans. Shahram T. Shiva, *Rending the Veil: Literal and Poetic Translations of Rumi* (Prescott, AZ: Hohm Press, 1995), p. 103.

About Second Journey

Second Journey is among a small number of emerging social-change organizations within the United States helping birth a new vision of the rich possibilities of later life. Our series of regional VISIONING COUNCILS on the topic Creating Community in Later Life has sparked creative, innovative thinking and led to the emergence of a national network of activists committed "to collectively dreaming the myths and creating the models that will galvanize social change."

Among the new possibilities glimpsed for later life are:

- an opportunity to open new avenues for individual growth and spiritual deepening;

- an opportunity to birth a renewed ethic of service and mentoring in later life; and

- an opportunity to marshal the distilled wisdom and experience of elders to address the converging crises of our time, both geopolitical and ecological.

Captured in the shorthand of our logo...

Mindfulness, Service, and Community in the Second Half of Life.

www.SecondJourney.org

Made in the USA
Lexington, KY
13 February 2011